The Snow Maiden and Other Russian Tales

World Folklore Series Advisory Board

THE SNOW MAIDEN AND OTHER RUSSIAN TALES

Translated and Retold by Bonnie C. Marshall

World Folklore Series

LIBRARIES
UNLIMITED
A Member of the Greenwood Publishing Group

Westport, Connecticut • London

3 1969 01560 3086

Library of Congress Cataloging-in-Publication Data is available at www.loc.gov.

British Library Cataloguing in Publication Data is available.

ISBN: 1–56308–999–8

First published in 2004

Libraries Unlimited, 88 Post Road West, Westport, CT 06881
A Member of the Greenwood Publishing Group, Inc.
www.lu.com

Printed in the United States of America

The paper used in this book complies with the
Permanent Paper Standard issued by the National
Information Standards Organization (Z39.48–1984).

10 9 8 7 6 5 4 3 2 1

The publisher has done its best to make sure the instructions and/or recipes in this book are cor-
rect. However, users should apply judgment and experience when preparing recipes, especially parents and teachers working with young people. The publisher accepts no responsibility for the
outcome of any recipe included in this volume.

The Snow Maiden and Other Russian Tales *is dedicated to my children and their spouses—Lorrie Carey and Paul Matthews and Peter and Heather Carey. It is dedicated, too, to the third generation of tale-spinners, my grandchildren Monica, Morgan, and MacNeil Matthews, and Skyler Carey.*

Recent Titles in the
World Folklore Series

Additional titles in this series can be found at www.lu.com

CONTENTS

Part 4: Tales of Spirits and the Supernatural

PREFACE

Until the fall of the Soviet Union, Russia was considered a strange and distant land, hidden behind "the iron curtain," and cloaked in mystery. Cold War policies maintained and exacerbated the image. Only a privileged few Americans were permitted entry to the Soviet Union, either as tourists, scholars on exchange programs, or diplomats and state department workers. Even these favored individuals were allowed only a peek behind the iron curtain, for they were limited in the possibility of arranging contacts with Russians and could travel only forty kilometers from the area stipulated in their visas. Foreigners were closely watched by the KGB and its informants (*stukachi*).

In 1975, I visited Russia as a participant in the IREX (International Research and Exchanges Board) Summer Exchange of Language Teachers. I lived in Moscow and attended Moscow State University. Leonid Brezhnev (1964–1982) was in power, and it was the height of *zastoi* (stagnation). The Soviet Union and its citizens seemed frozen in time, asleep in a petrified kingdom untouched by the flow of information and progress. Before our group left the United States, a State Department representative warned us not to fraternize with the Russians, an order that seemed somehow to defeat the purpose of a cultural exchange. Our Soviet hosts received similar orders from their government.

I met Alla Vasil'evna Kulagina, who served as advisor for this book, in the summer of 1975 when I attended her folklore seminar at Moscow State University. Our ensuing friendship and collaboration bear witness to the fact that governments cannot separate kindred spirits. I approached folklore through my interest in children's literature. My Moscow adventures, the seminar, and my exposure to folklore texts and recordings from the university archives marked a new stage in my academic career. I decided to specialize in the study of Russian folklore. Folklore, in turn, led me straight to the heart and spirit of the people of Russia, with whom I have had a long-standing love affair.

In 1978–1979, I returned to the Soviet Union and to Moscow State University (MGU), thanks again to IREX, to work on my dissertation, "Typological Models of the Heroine in the Russian Fairy Tale" (The University of North Carolina, 1983). In those days research was controlled and restricted, but I was determined to do some fieldwork in addition to perusing material in the Lenin Library. My naïve suggestion that I accompany MGU students on a folklore expedition into the countryside astounded Nikolai I. Kravtsov, then Chair of the Department of Folklore. Nevertheless, I was permitted to audit a class conducted by Professor Vladimir Prokop'evich Anikin. Surreptitiously, I began the forbidden task of collecting urban folklore, which consisted of popular ditties called *chastushki* and anecdotes, a few of which appear in the introduction to this book.

Alla V. Kulagina and I kept in touch throughout the passing years. In 1985, when I participated in another teachers' exchange, located this time in Leningrad, Alla traveled from Moscow to Leningrad with her small son Sasha to visit. Not one hotel in the city would accommodate a woman with a child, nor was Alla permitted to use the extra space in my room for fear of having her internal passport confiscated by hotel personnel. She and Sasha had to return to Moscow the same day on the "Red Arrow" train.

Although I returned several times to the Soviet Union under the auspices of the American Council of Teachers of Russian (ACTR), it was not until 1991, the year that communism fell, that I finally was able to do fieldwork in Russia. The following year, in 1992, Alla made her first visit to the United States. We worked together on a bilingual folklore text that is in production at Moscow State University.

In subsequent years, I taught English at the School for Global Education in St. Petersburg (formerly Leningrad) and at the American Academy of Foreign Languages in Moscow. I was able to witness the process of democratization and the development of an intriguing cowboy capitalism. One of my most unnerving and Kafkaesque experiences was teaching English to Russian businessmen under armed guard. Personal, armed body guards were present to protect the businessmen from assassination and violence.

These assignments have allowed Alla and me to continue our collaboration, of which this collection of folktales is a product. It is our desire to introduce American children, parents, teachers, and lovers of folklore to some of Russia's most beloved tales, known to every Russian child. In addition, we have added a type of tale known as the *bylichka* (memorate), which has been neglected by Soviet scholarship and has only recently begun to receive the attention it deserves. We believe that this collection fills a gap in the literature, and we hope that you will enjoy reading and sharing the stories as much as we have enjoyed finding them.

ACKNOWLEDGMENTS

This project would not have been realized without the help of the International Research and Exchanges Board and the American Council of Teachers of Russian, both of which gave me the opportunity through grants to do research in Russia and to acquire the knowledge needed to complete the task. To Professors Alla V. Kulagina and Vladimir P. Anikin, I am profoundly grateful for offering guidance, knowledge, and consultations, even during the Soviet era when it was dangerous for them to do so. To Professor Charles Zug of The University of North Carolina at Chapel Hill, I am indebted for a general knowledge of folklore, an acquaintance with American theory and methodology, and for encouragement.

For recipes and culinary lessons, as well as for exposure to the color and richness of the Russian language, I am grateful to Zina Nikitina. To Marianna Shabat, Vera Serebrianikova, Margaret Coleman of Boston's Russian-American Cultural Center, Sasha Matveev, Tatiana Mamonova, and Professors Rimma Teremova, Rochelle Ruthchild, Eleazar Meletinskii, and Ludmilla Leibman, I am indebted for materials, encouragement, and inspiration.

A special debt of gratitude is owed to my editor Barbara Ittner for her wisdom, guidance, and enthusiastic promotion of Slavic folklore.

INTRODUCTION

Geography

Russia is an impressive country, if only for its sheer vastness. When Russia was the Union of Soviet Socialist Republics (1922–1991), it occupied one-sixth of the earth's surface. Even after losing the breakaway republics on its borders, the nation still encompasses an area almost twice the size of the United States. Eleven time zones pass through its borders. Russia stretches from Finland, Latvia, Estonia, Lithuania, Belarus, and Ukraine in the west through Siberia to the Pacific Ocean in the east. It extends from the Arctic Ocean in the north to Mongolia, China, Kazakhstan, Azerbaijan, and Georgia in the south. In terms of geographic area, it is the largest country in the world.

The Ural Mountains divide European and Asian Russia, so that Russia extends over two continents and is part of both Europe and northern Asia. West of the Urals lies the Eastern European Plain. Siberia lies between the Ural Mountains and the Pacific Ocean.

Rivers and bodies of water have played an important role in Russia's history and economy. The most famous river in Russia is the Volga. This mighty river flows 2,290 miles into the Caspian Sea, an inland saltwater sea located between Europe and Asia. Other important rivers in Russia include the Don, Ob, Yenisei, and the Lena. Lake Baikal—the deepest lake in the world—can be found in southeastern Siberia.

No description of Russia is complete without mention of its two most important cities, Moscow and St. Petersburg. Moscow is the capital city and serves as the seat of government. It is Russia's cultural and intellectual center, although St. Petersburgers would take issue with that statement and point to grander days when St. Peterburg was Russia's capital and the heart of its intellectual ferment and progress. Moscow is located in the Eastern European Lowlands between the Smolensk Hills to the north and the Central Russian Plain to the south. Its population is over nine million.[1] At its heart is the Kremlin, a walled fortress that at one time enclosed the entire city. The Kremlin contains palaces, government buildings, the State Armory, towers, and churches.

St. Petersburg is Russia's second largest city and one of Europe's most beautiful. Referred to as the "Venice of the North," it has come full circle in its change of name. It was founded in 1703 by Peter the Great and was named St. Petersburg after him. During World War I its name was changed to Petrograd. Later, it was named Leningrad after

The SOVIET UNION Included RUSSIA and Its Breakaway Republics

Latvia
Lithuania
Estonia
Russia
Belarus
Ukraine
Moldova
Georgia
Armenia
Azerbaijan
Russia
Kazakhstan
Kyrgyzstan
Tajikistan
Turkmenistan
Uzbekistan

N

Soviet Names

Russia (Russian Federated Soviet Socialist Republic)
Belarus (White Russian S.S.R.)
Ukraine (Ukrainian S.S.R.)
Armenia (Armenian S.S.R.)
Azerbaijan (Azerbaijan S.S.R.)

Estonia (Estonian S.S.R.)
Georgia (Georgian S.S.R.)
Kazakhstan (Kazakh S.S.R)
Kyrgyzstan (Kirgiz S.S.R.)
Latvia (Latvian S.S.R.)
Lithuania (Lituanian S.S.R.)

Moldova (Moldavian S.S.R.)
Tajikistan (Tajik S.S. R.)
Turkmenistan (Turkmen S.S.R.)
Uzbekistan (Uzbek S.S.R.)

Russia and its former republics.

Physical Map of RUSSIA

Svalbard **(NORWAY)**

NORWAY

SWEDEN

FINLAND

POLAND

EST.

LAT.

LITH.

RUS.

BALTIC SEA

BELARUS

UKRAINE

Lake Ladoga

Lake Onega

Moscow

Volga River

Don River

BLACK SEA

TURKEY

ARM.

GEO.

AZER.

IRAN

CASPIAN SEA

TURK-MENISTAN

UZBEK-ISTAN

ARAL SEA

KAZAKHSTAN

BARENTS SEA

Novaia Zemlia

Severnaia Zemlia

KARA SEA

Franz Josef Land

LAPTEV SEA

New Siberian Islands

Lake Taymyr

ARCTIC OCEAN

Wrangel Island

CHUKCHI SEA

EAST SIBERIAN SEA

St. Lawrence Island **(U.S.)**

BERING SEA

PACIFIC OCEAN

Kam-chatka

Koriakskoe Plateau

Chukotskoe Plateau

Kolyma River

Range of Cherskogo

Kolymskoe Plateau

Kuril Islands

SEA OF OKHOTSK

Sakhalin Island

TATAR STRAIT

Amur River

JAPAN

SEA OF JAPAN

N. KOREA

S. KOREA

CHINA

MONGOLIA

CHINA

Yana River

Suntar-Khaiata Range

Verkhovianskii Range

Lena River

Aldan River

Aldanskoe Plateau

Dzhugdzhur Range

Stanovoi Range

Yablonovyi Range

Stanovoe Plateau

Lake Baikal

Central Siberian Plateau

Yenisei River

Lena River

Sayan Mountains

Altai Mountains

West Siberian Plain

Ob River

Irtysh River

Ob River

S I B E R I A

URALS

Eastern European Plain

Physical map of Russia.

A Leningrad courtyard in rubble in 1990, just before the fall of the Soviet Union, stands as a symbol of failed communism.

Vladimir Ilyich Lenin, the founder of Soviet communism. After communism fell in 1991, the name reverted to St. Petersburg.

Russia's landscape is as varied as its size might suggest. In the far north we find the Arctic permafrost and tundra. Despite the extreme cold, this area sustains life. The moss, bushes, and lichen of the tundra give way to pines and birches in its southern reaches. Below the tundra stretches the taiga, or boreal coniferous forest, with its magnificent evergreens. South of the taiga lies the steppe. There, forests combine with grasslands and eventually give way to flat land with feather grass.

History

Russian history is full of dramatic, sometimes tragic, events that make it a colorful and absorbing story. The following overview is not intended to provide a thorough history of the country, but to give readers a basic understanding of the country's past, and to offer them a glimpse of a mysterious and exciting part of the world.

Origins and Kievan Russia

The first mystery one encounters when studying Russian history involves the origins of the Slavs. Russians belong to the Slavic branch of the Indo-European ethno-linguistic group. Scholars have theorized that the homeland of the Slavs lies in the valley of the Vistula River and in the Carpathian Mountains. According to this theory, in the sixth century A.D. the Slavs split into three groups: the East Slavs, who migrated north to lands where people of Finnic and Lithuanian origin lived and inhabited the Eastern European Plain; the West Slavs, who became the modern Poles, Czechs, and Slovaks; and the South Slavs, who settled in modern Bulgaria and the Balkans. This theory has come under criticism and been rejected by most scholars because of recent archeological findings that indicate that the Slavs existed much earlier, during Scythian times.[2]

The Kievan state (860–1240) emerged as a Slavic center of power and culture. Its inhabitants were called Rus'. The name "Russian" evolved from the word Rus'.

The Russian *Primary Chronicle*, an annal that contains a description of important historical, religious, and political events, states that the Scandinavian Rus' (Vikings) were invited to rule the Slavs in the year 862. Although the *Primary Chronicle* is not a reliable historical source, but rather a compilation of legends, folklore, lives of the saints and princes, and history, where fact and fantasy are combined, it is our chief source of information on early Russian culture.[3]

In 987, during the reign of Prince Vladimir I (978–1015), the Kievan Rus' were converted to Christianity. The *Primary Chronicle* relates that Prince Vladimir embraced Greek, or Eastern, Orthodoxy because his envoys told him that being in the ornate and beautiful Orthodox Church made them feel as if they were in heaven. Indeed, the Russian Orthodox Church was modeled after the Greek model, with an impressive dome, frequently blue in color, that transports the worshipper in thought to heaven, thereby providing a welcome contrast to stark reality.

The lack of a clear line of succession resulted in the Kievan state's break up into several principalities, each with its own prince. Disagreements and conflicts weakened the state and made it vulnerable to invaders.

In 1240, Mongols of the Golden Horde, Central Asian nomads under the leadership of Genghis Khan, conquered Kiev. From 1240 to 1480 Kievan Russia and its extended principalities languished under Mongol and Tatar rule. The Rus' were forced to pay tribute to the Horde and to serve in the Mongol army.

It was not until 1380, when Moscow Prince Dmitrii Donskoi defeated the Mongols in the Battle of Kulikovo Field, that the tide turned back in favor of the Russians. Yet another hundred years passed before Ivan III of Moscow was able to completely renounce Russian servitude to the khan.

Tsarist Russia

Ivan IV (1530–1584), known as Ivan the Terrible, expanded Russia into Siberia. Ivan the Terrible declared himself the "Tsar and Grand Prince Ivan of all Russia."[4] In folklore Ivan IV is generally depicted as a caring protector of his people, although in fact he had a cruel nature. His reign was marked by violence, and thus he acquired the nickname of the Terrible (*groznyi*). With his dreaded elite unit, the *oprichina*, he terrorized the country and killed every suspected enemy, including his son and heir Ivan Tsarevich, leaving the country without a competent successor upon his death.

From 1598 to 1613, a period of political upheaval called the Time of Trouble (*Smutnoe vremia*) ensued. When Ivan the Terrible's weak son Feodor I proved to be incompetent, Feodor's brother-in-law Boris Godunov took over; and upon Feodor's death he became ruler. Godunov was suspected of having killed Tsarevich Dmitrii, Feodor's brother. Pretenders to the throne, supported by Poland and pretending to be Dmitrii, began appearing. Both peasants and boyars, members of the privileged aristocracy, were unhappy, and a civil war that lasted almost a decade ensued. Upon Godunov's death, the false Dmitrii was made tsar, only to be rapidly replaced by boyar Vasilii Shuiskii, who was in turn overthrown.

It was not until the Romanov dynasty came to power that Russia regained stability. This dynasty ruled Russia from 1613 to 1917. The first of the line was Mikhail Romanov (1613–1645).

Peter I (1672–1725), or Peter the Great, was one of the most notable Romanovs. He was even offered the title of Emperor. Peter I expanded the empire and moved the capital from Moscow to St. Petersburg. Despite the resistance of many members of the aristocracy, he modernized Russia, reforming the government with Western models in mind and traveling to Europe to learn how to do so. He improved the army and navy so that at Peter's death Russia had one of the largest armies in Europe.[5] He forced men to shave their beards, encouraged foreign study, and gave his court lessons in social etiquette. In 1722 he created a Table of Ranks for the military and civil servants. By the end of the Great Northern War (1700–1721) and Russia's victory over Sweden, Russia was firmly entrenched in the Baltic.

Not long after the death of Peter I, another important ruler came to power—Catherine II (1729 to 1796), also known as Catherine the Great. Catherine II ruled from 1762 to 1796. Her reign was long and she became legendary, but her personal beliefs conflicted with her policies. Ultimately, her captivating image is more important than her actual accomplishments.[6] Although Catherine II purported to believe in progressive, revolutionary ideas, she placed the church under state control and she was merciless in quelling rebellions, such as that of Don Cossack Emelian Pugachev, whom she had executed in 1775. She extended serfdom to areas in Ukraine where the system had not previously existed; and by drawing up the Charter of the Nobility, she created a class system that decreased the peasants' powers. Nevertheless, by promoting French culture and language and strengthening education, she ushered in an age of Russian Enlightenment.

After Catherine the Great died, her son, Paul I (1754–1801), who despised his mother, purposely reversed her policies. Catherine had intended to join Austria against the French revolutionary government, but Paul I abandoned her plans. The situation worsened until June 1812 when, during the reign of Alexander I (1777–1825), Napoleon invaded Russia. Napoleon's soldiers had inadequate supplies and suffered from poor morale.[7] Russian peasants willingly burned their homes and crops rather than aid the French by supplying them with food. Ultimately, Napoleon had no choice but to retreat, but he made the unfortunate choice of October as the departure date. During the severe Russian winter, his army of 600,000 was reduced to somewhere between 30,000 to 50,000 men.[8]

The next Russian leader, Nicholas I (1796–1855), was noted for his repressive conservatism. On December 26, 1825, as he was assuming power, the Decembrists, a group of liberal members of the military and aristocracy, revolted against Alexander I's increasingly regressive policies. The event is important because it was a revolutionary protest against the regime perpetrated not by peasants, but by the upper classes.

In 1853, the Ottoman Empire declared war on Russia and was joined by England and France. Known as the Crimean War, it ended in 1856 during the reign of Alexander II, Nicholas's son, in a resounding defeat for Russia. In the subsequent Treaty of Paris, Russia lost her southern territory. In the course of his reign, Alexander II (1818–1881) made liberal reforms, the most notable of which was the emancipation of the serfs in 1861. Nevertheless, the emancipation was considered inadequate by members of the People's Will, whose assassination of Alexander II in 1881 ironically resulted in the death of Russia's most liberal tsar.

Nicholas II (1868–1917), Alexander II's son, was a personable family man who was incapable of ruling Russia. His wife Alexandra became the real power behind the throne. She was aided by a peasant named Gregorii Rasputin, whose whimsical advice ruined the last Romanovs. Two events contributed to malcontent among the people. The first event was Bloody Sunday (1905), during which a group of workers, led by Father Gapon and carrying the tsar's portrait, walked toward the Winter Palace and were massacred. The second event was World War I, in which Russia suffered heavy losses. On March 15, 1917, the incompetent Nicholas II was persuaded to abdicate. He and his family were exiled by the Bolsheviks to Yekaterinburg, where they were subsequently executed.

The Russian Revolution

After the abdication of Nicholas II, the Provisional Government, which supported democracy, was established with Alexander Kerensky as Prime Minister. But later that year, on November 7, 1917, the Provisional Government was defeated by a revolutionary coup of the Bolshevik (Communist) Party, led by Vladimir Ilyich Lenin (1870–1924). Lenin's motley band of soldiers, sailors, and workers stormed the Winter Palace in Petrograd (St. Petersburg). Influenced by the philosophy of Karl Marx, Lenin ordered the seizure of land and factories for impoverished workers and peasants, resulting in the nationalization of property with the government as owner.

The Soviet Era

Communism and the so-called "dictatorship of the proletariat" lasted for seventy-four years, from 1917 to 1991. In 1922, Russia became known as the Union of Soviet Socialist Republics. The government was centralized, which resulted in the creation of a slow, ineffective bureaucracy. Religions were prohibited, and atheism was proclaimed. In reality, what evolved was a pseudo-religion with Lenin as god. Edicts were enforced cruelly and violently by a maniacal CHEKA (All-Russian Extraordinary Commission to Combat Counter-Revolution and Sabotage), precursor to the KGB, led by the dreaded Felix Dzerzhinsky. The anecdote below makes a subtle criticism of the regime and an allusion to the fear in which it was held.[9] Open criticism resulted in imprisonment.

> Scientists found out how to reanimate the dead and resurrected Lenin. Lenin requested that he be given three days to inspect the country's situation. He was given the three days and disappeared without a trace. Then the scientists resurrected Dzerzhinsky and sent him in search of Lenin. Suddenly, Dzerzhinsky received a telegram from

Former KGB building and pedestal of a monument that was toppled in 1991. The monument had been erected to honor Felix Dzerzhinsky (1877–1926), head of the Soviet CHEKA and OGPU (Unified State Political Administration).

Switzerland. It said: "Fly here right away, and we'll start over from the beginning. Lenin."[10]

The Civil War, War Communism, and the New Economic Policy

From 1918 to 1921 Russia experienced a civil war in which Reds, who supported Lenin and the revolution, battled and conquered Whites, supporters of tsarism and the old regime. Under the policies of War Communism, the urban worker and poor peasant were favored over other members of society, such as merchants, intellectuals, and wealthy peasants (known as *kulaks*). Well-to-do peasants were divested of food at fixed prices so that the Red Army could be fed. In 1921 a famine swept the country. Many people died, and others moved to the country in hopes of feeding their families off the land. In 1921 Lenin instituted a compromise to capitalism, called the New Economic Policy, on a temporary basis. It represented a relaxation of policies that resulted in a much-needed economic improvement.

Stalin, the Five-Year Plans, and World War II

After Lenin's death in 1924, Joseph Stalin (1879–1953) seized power after ruthlessly murdering his rivals. He set up an absolute dictatorship. So-called "enemies of the state" were "purged," i.e., executed, exiled, or sent to labor camps. Free expression was prohibited. During the Great Purges of the 1930s, neighbors spied on one another seeking phantasmagoric enemies, as the anecdote below demonstrates.

A Soviet citizen informed the KGB (Committee of State Security) that his Jewish neighbor in the apartment next door wanted to emigrate. The KGB agent interrogated the Jew and asked him why he wanted to leave the country.

> *"There are two reasons I want to leave the Soviet Union," he said.*
> *"What are they?" asked the KGB agent.*
> *"The first reason is that my neighbor keeps saying the Soviet regime will fall."*
> *"That's ridiculous!" said the agent. "Why do you pay any attention to him? The Soviet regime will never fall."*
> *"That's the second reason I want to emigrate," said the Jew.*

Under Stalin, the Soviet Union underwent a transformation to an industrialized society that rivaled the United States. With his Five-Year Plans, Stalin set goals for industrial and military growth. Unwilling peasants were herded into collectives and state farms (*sovkhozy*), all at the cost of great human suffering. Writers, artists, scientists, architects, composers—professional people—were enlisted in the service of building communism and spewed stereotypical nonsense to please the state. Real talent often went unnoticed, or worse, punished.

In 1939 the Soviet Union signed nonaggression and neutrality treaties with Nazi Germany and Japan. Nevertheless, Hitler invaded Russia in the summer of 1940 and declared war a year later. In 1941 the Soviet Union joined the allies against the German axis, and World War II, known in Russia as the Great Patriotic War, resulted in staggering losses.

The Cold War Era

During World War II, the Soviet Union and the West formed an alliance, but as time passed differences resulted in distrust and hostility. The Cold War era set in. After the death of Stalin in 1953, a period of thaw brought hope when Nikita Khrushchev (1894–1964) assumed power as First Secretary and gave an anti-Stalin speech at the Twentieth Party Congress in 1956. However, intellectuals were disappointed with the amount of artistic expression allowed, and they noted that not a great deal had changed, as the anecdote below shows.

> *Question: What would happen if you cried out in Red Square, "Nikita [Khrushchev] is a fool"?*
> *Answer: You'd get twenty-five years in prison—five years for criticizing Khrushchev and twenty years for revealing a state secret.*

Satellite nations, which the Soviet Union had forced into its camp, began rebelling and were brutally suppressed (Hungary in 1957 and Czechoslovakia in 1968). The country's energy focused on military and space achievements.[11]

Khrushchev was replaced by a series of ineffectual leaders, bureaucrats at heart, who attempted to hold back change. Leonid Brezhnev, who ruled from 1964 to 1982, was one of the Soviet Union's more memorable leaders. Under his rule, the living standards of the ordinary Soviet citizen improved without any real reform. During his final days, his mental deterioration became so apparent that anecdotes accentuating his senility began circulating.

> *Brezhnev asked his ghostwriters to compose a twenty-minute speech. He was handed a pile of papers, and he started reading. The reading lasted three hours. Angry, he called his writers and scolded them for writing a three-hour speech when he had requested a twenty-minute speech.*

His amazed writers said, "We gave you the speech and eight copies of the speech.
You have read the same speech nine times."

It was not until Mikhail Gorbachev became General Secretary in 1985 that reform was effected and democratization and freedom finally came to the Soviet Union. Gorbachev advocated *glasnost'* (openness), which allowed freedom of expression and religious freedom, and *perestroika* (restructuring of the country and the Soviet system) to save the country from economic ruin and from ethnic unrest. Initially supported for his policies by the liberal segment of the population, Gorbachev eventually caused disenchantment among the people. Liberals criticized him for taking halfway measures and moving slowly, and conservatives opposed his reforms and the speed with which he instituted them. The more people suffered economically, the more disgruntled they grew. Ultimately, Gorbachev was more popular in the West than in his own country.

The Fall of the Soviet Union and the Post-Soviet Era

In 1991 Gorbachev resigned following a failed coup led by Prime Minister Valentin Pavlov, Vice President Gennadii Yanev, and other hard-line conservatives. After seventy-four years of Soviet rule, the Soviet Union ceased to exist. When Russia, Ukraine, and Kazakhstan declared their independence, followed by the Baltic republics, Belarus, Georgia, Azerbaijan, Turkmenistan, Uzbekistan, Moldova, Armenia, Kyrgyzstan, and Tajikistan, it became a loose confederation of republics named the Commonwealth of Independent States.

President Boris Yeltsin, who led Russia from 1992 to 2000, defended Gorbachev during the coup, and he later became the first democratically elected leader. Yeltsin's regime was fraught with crises and problems. His attempts at rapid reform resulted in a growing opposition. That opposition escalated when Yeltsin dissolved the parliament on September 22, 1993, and a bloodbath ensued when Russian citizens defended conservative parliament members, who had barricaded themselves in the parliament building. It is estimated that 140 people were killed in the ensuing struggle.[12]

In 1994 Russian troops, grossly underpaid and demoralized, were sent to Chechnya to quell the Chechens' independence movement. The war ended in 1997, but in the years that have followed, trouble in this area has continued. In recent years, Chechen rebels have employed terrorist tactics against Russia and they have claimed responsibility for several bombings in Moscow. Yeltsin faced other ethnic crises when the autonomous regions in Russia began demanding independence in the mid-1990s.

The country was also beset with economic woes. In 1998, Russia defaulted on all payments, and the bank system was frozen. The ruble, Russia's monetary unit, retained only twenty-five percent of its value. Yeltsin's health deteriorated, and he underwent by-pass surgery. Shortly thereafter, he began dismissing his prime ministers and cabinet members. Russia and the United States disagreed over the war in Kosovo, with Russia supporting the Serbs. Yeltsin was also challenged by a powerful Russian Mafia that had managed to infiltrate the government and business. The Mafia became notorious for assassinating bankers and for demanding protection money (*krysha*) from businesses.

On December 31, 1999, Yeltsin resigned, naming Vladimir Putin as his replacement. In March 2000 Putin was elected president. Putin has grappled with the continuation of the economic and ethnic problems of Yeltsin's regime. Although Russia gained control of Grozny, the Chechen capital, in February 2000, Chechen terrorist tactics have not ceased.

A memorial outside the Parliament building to a young protester who was killed during the near-civil war that erupted in 1993. It reads: Mama, forgive me. They killed me for loving my native land.

On October 23, 2002, Chechen terrorists took over a Moscow theater during a musical performance and, threatening to bomb the building, held hostage an audience of over 800 people. In rescue maneuvers by the Russian army, 116 people died.[13]

Russian Life

Russia's total population has been given variously as 147 million (in 1995) according to ACTR's *Cultural Handbook to the New Independent States*; as 148,179,000 (in 1999) in Minton F. Goldman's *Russia, the Eurasian Republics, and Central/European Europe*; and as 144,978,573 in the 2003 *World Almanac and Book of Facts*. Not only does the last figure indicate no population gain, but it also indicates an actual loss of population. Men living in Russia have an average life expectancy of 62.3 years and women live on the average to 73, according to the 2003 *World Almanac and Book of Facts*. That is an improvement over what the *World Almanac* recorded two years earlier. In 2001 it gave 59.06 as the average lifespan of men and 71.8 as the average lifespan for women. These statistics apply to all 108 peoples living in Russia, of which ethnic Russians, whose folktales we will explore, form the majority (81.5 percent).[14]

Russian, a Slavic language, is written in Cyrillic letters. The ancestor of the Russian alphabet was created by Greek missionaries, brothers Cyril and Methodius. Therefore, many letters resemble Greek ones.

The Russian's nature is warm, straightforward, expansive, and accepting of fate. Traditionally, Russians have shown concern about others, even strangers on the street, and are very helpful. They form lasting friendships. The ordinary Russian is not wealthy. According to the 2003 *World Almanac* the per capita income is equivalent to $7,700 a year. Most pensioners receive less than $100 a month.[15] Many Russians have a summer house (*dacha*), where they grow vegetables to supplement their food supply. The poverty of most

Russians contrasts with the extreme wealth of the New Russians, an emerging class of businessmen and Mafia bosses, as the anecdote below demonstrates.

> *Two New Russians arrived at an automobile dealership to buy two Mercedes-600s.*
> *First New Russian: "Stop, I'll pay for both our cars."*
> *Second New Russian: "But why should you pay?"*
> *First New Russian: "Well, after all, you treated me to a meal in a café yesterday.*
> *It's my turn to treat you."*

Older Russians often complain that capitalism is slowly eroding the Russian character, and that young people have less concern about their fellowmen than do members of the older generation. They claim that young people are focused on themselves and getting ahead, whereas under communism the collective good took precedence over the needs and desires of the individual.

Russians today still enjoy gathering at friends' homes around a table laden with food. They are capable of sitting until dawn conversing, telling anecdotes, singing songs, and reciting four-lined ditties called *chastushki*. The typical ritual consists of eating appetizers (*zakuski*) while drinking vodka. Numerous toasts are made. The toast has developed into an art form. Appetizers are followed by soup, such as cabbage soup (*shchi*) or borsch. The meat dish might be chicken cutlets (*kotlety*), shashlik, or beef stroganoff, accompanied by various salads. Desert might consist of sponge cake (*keks*), ice cream, or napoleons.

Russians enjoy walking through the forest and vacationing at resorts (*kuroty*). Vacations were free in Soviet times, but under communism the ordinary Russian was not al-

Around a Russian table.

Mumming (dressing up in costumes and masks) is part of the New Year's tradition.

lowed to travel freely to other countries, and it is only within the past decade that Russians have begun to explore the world.

In the past, New Year's Eve was the most celebrated Soviet holiday, and it remains a very important day. Guests arrive to the traditional table, and an all-night party ensues. When the Kremlin bells chime, everyone toasts the new year. There is a New Year's tree (*elka*) and gifts are exchanged, albeit on a smaller scale than in the United States at Christmas, the western holiday most closely resembling the Russian New Year. Grandfather Frost (*Ded Moroz*) and his helper, the Snow Maiden (*Snegurochka*), appear at the children's New Year Party, during which the children encircle the tree and dance and sing.

Now that religious beliefs are no longer discouraged as they were in communist times, Christmas (January 7) and Easter are growing in popularity. The night before Easter, worshippers bring eggs, *kulich* (cylindrical bread), and *paskha* (a kind of cheesecake) to church to be blessed. At midnight the priest leads a procession around the church, symbolically reenacting Mary Magdelene's search for Jesus's body. After the return to church, symbolizing the opening of the tomb, the priest announces that "Christ is risen!" The congregation replies, "He is truly risen!" After church, fasting is broken and followed by a long, celebratory feast.

Independence Day (June 12) is a new holiday that celebrates the creation of the new Russian state. There are parades and fireworks. November 7, Russian Revolution Day, which was never a very happy holiday, has lost its significance and is largely ignored. On March 8, International Women's Day, men give women gifts and flowers. Unlike our Mother's Day, women do not have to be mothers to be recognized and appreciated. Men are remembered, although not as widely, on Army and Navy Day (February 23).

May Day festivities in Moscow, 1993.

May 1, International Workers' Day, was always an enjoyable holiday, a celebration of spring, and it remains so.

The Tales

History of Russian Folklore

After the Christianization of Russia in 987, the clergy fought pagan beliefs and oral traditions. Nevertheless, religious scribes made chance references to these traditions in church literature and annals, which remain to this day the source of our knowledge about pagan gods, rituals, beliefs, legends, songs, and tales. Only in the seventeenth century did the recording of folklore begin, when two Englishmen, Richard James and Samuel Collins, compiled historical songs and folktales from the Archangelsk area.[16]

In the eighteenth century, the Russian nobility overtly regarded oral literature as inferior and déclassé. However, among the peasantry it flourished. In contradiction to their expressed disdain for folk traditions, the nobility, too, was involved in staging theatrical presentations featuring peasant songs and peasant actors, and was entertained by folktales. Poet Aleksandr Pushkin, for example, credited his beloved nurse Arina Rodionovna with instilling in him a love of poetry and the folk with her taletelling. By the late eighteenth century Vasilii A. Levshin published ten volumes of *Russian Tales, Containing the Most Ancient Narratives of the Renowned Knights, Popular Tales, and Others Surviving Through the Retelling of Adventures* (1780–1783). The lower classes were entertained by the inexpensive *lubok*, a chapbook with little text and large woodcut prints.

In the nineteenth century, a worldwide interest in folklore arose in connection with the emergence of the Romantic Movement, with its emphasis on nature, feeling, creativity, idealism, the common man, and national spirit. In Germany, the brothers Wilhelm (1787–1859) and Jakob (1785–1863) Grimm collected and published tales, thereby promoting the idealization of German traditions. In Russia, Aleksandr N. Afanas'ev (1826–1871) played a role similar to that of the Grimm brothers, and his name is synonymous with the concept of Russian folklore. His multivolume collection of *Russian Folk Tales* (*Narodnye russkie skazki*) was published between 1855 and 1863. Other collections he published include *Russian Legends* (*Narodnye russkie legendy*, 1859) and *Russian Secret Tales* (*Russkie zavetnye skazki*, 1872).

Afanas'ev and the Grimms espoused the theories of the mythological school, which linked folklore to myths. The mythological school represented the beginning of the scientific study of folklore in Russia, to which Afanas'ev contributed an influential volume entitled *The Poetic Views of the Slavs on Nature* (*Poèticheskie vozzreniia slavian na prirodu*, 1865–1869) describing and comparing pagan beliefs with nineteenth-century traditions.

Other tale collectors followed in Afanas'ev's footsteps. They include Dmitrii N. Sadovnikov, who published tales he collected in the Samara area in 1884; N. E. Onchukov, whose *Northern Tales* came out in 1909; and D. K. Zelenin, whose tales from the Perm and Vyatka areas were published in 1915. That same year Boris and Yurii Sokolov published *Tales and Songs of the Belozerskii Region*. A. M. Smirnov was responsible for the publication in 1917 of tales that had accumulated in the archives of the Russian Geographical Society after the publication of Afanas'ev's collection.

The German scholar Theodor Benfey formed the theory that tales are borrowed among various peoples. This theory emphasized the similarities of stories found in various cultures due to borrowings, particularly from the East. In Russia, this theory was popular with the Orientalists and students of Siberian and Eastern folklore. Its major proponents were Aleksandr Nikolaevich Veselovskii (1837–1906), who was interested in cultural connections and who broadened Benfey's work, and V. J. Miller, who studied the heroic epic (*bylina*).

Related to Benfey's theory of borrowings is the Finnish School. In Scandinavia Kaarle Krohn (1863–1933) began what became known as the Finnish School. The folklorists of this school tackled the task of creating a subject index of tales, in which folktales were classified according to their traits and motifs. They hoped to create a system with which folklorists could trace the routes by which tales migrated from country to country. Krohn's student Antii Aarne published just such a tale-type index in 1910 (*Verzeichnis der Märchentypen mit Hülfe von Fachgenossen ausgearbeitet von Antii Aarne*). In 1929 in Russia, N. P. Andreev translated into Russian and enlarged Aarne's index; and in 1961 in the United States, Stith Thompson translated into English and enlarged Aarne's index. This index has been, and continues to be, an invaluable tool for the study of the folktale. Nevertheless, in 1936 at a Leningrad conference of the Academy of Sciences, the works of N. P. Andreev and the Finnish School were publicly discredited by puppets of the Communist Party.

The concrete and literally minded historical school, which emphasized the dating, geographical location, and actual facts connected to specimens of oral literature, arose in reaction to idealistic and effusive romanticism. The historical school remained in vogue until the Russian Revolution of 1917. Although the historical school took into consideration the content of folk creations, it largely ignored their artistic aspects. This school fell into disfavor with the Soviets because of its so-called "sociological speculations," i.e., its insistence on the aristocratic origin of folklore because folktales and epic poems (*byliny*) were peopled with tsars and tsarevnas, nobles, wealthy merchants, and the like. Folklorist Yurii Sokolov fell victim to criticism on this score. These ideas ran afoul of the Soviet government's plan to use folklore to promote communism and to glorify the common man—the worker and the peasant—at the expense of the upper classes—the wealthy, cultured, and educated.

Adherents of the anthropological school, such as Bronislaw Malinowski and Franz Boas, studied primitive, isolated cultures and pointed out that there were as many differences as similarities between tales from different cultures. Yet another view was taken by adherents of the Freudian school, who read psychological meanings connected to sexual dysfunction into folktales. Others with a psychological bent favored the theories of Carl Jung (1875–1961) concerning the collective unconscious in the study and interpretation of folktales. Russian philologist N. Ia. Marr created a method of "paleontological analysis." He applied this method to linguistic data while integrating the findings of related fields, such as ethnography, archeology, and folkloristics. As a result, he was able to demonstrate the weakness of Indo-European comparative linguistics.

All of the above-mentioned schools were discredited by the Soviets, whose emphasis on the importance of the national and collective concept in work and scholarship was not served by the study of folktales from other cultures and in isolation, as the anthropological school advocates. Nor could Soviet doctrine sanction Freud's emphasis on sex and the internal life of the individual, while Jung's theories were virtually unknown to Soviet scholars. Even students of the respected Marr were criticized for narrowness of concept in their search for "survivals" of ancient times in folklore texts and for their alleged attempt to reduce all folklore to these "survivals."

The formalist school arose in opposition to the historical and anthropological schools. Despite the bleak climate for thought, Russian scholarship shone on the international horizon when Vladimir Propp, who emphasized the formal and artistic aspects of folktales, published his findings. He claimed that all fairy tales may be morphologically deduced from the basic one involving the abduction of the heroine by the villain.[17] However, the formalists, too, fell into disfavor in the Soviet Union because their focus on text, devices, structure, and aesthetics, rather than on the text as it relates to man, was considered an empty, idle "bourgeois" contemplation. At an Academy of Sciences conference in 1936, Propp was criticized for having formalistic principles. Indeed, the term "formalist" became pejorative and was used to censure any artist, scholar, or writer who went astray and deviated from the Soviet norm, which was known as socialist realism.

That norm involved using folklore and literature to further Communist Party values, ideals, and goals. Folklore became the handmaiden of the Party in service to communism. The situation was complicated because folklore itself was in transition. Formerly, collectors focused mainly on folktales and folk songs (especially the *bylina*). As these longer genres became less suited to the pace of life, and as books, radio, television, movies, and the like replaced tale-telling as a form of entertainment, as literacy grew, new genres became popular, such as the four-line *chastushka*, the modern joke, and the anecdote. The definition of folklore became blurred and many genres were studied that were not folklore at all, but instead were what American folklorist Richard M. Dorson referred to as "fakelore." Thus, workers and peasants began creating stories about Lenin and Stalin that were accepted as legitimate folklore. Soviet folklorists focused on themes concerning the beneficial influence of communism, country life, the economy, and the military as they were depicted in popular culture. Soviet folklorist K. V. Chistov took an extreme stance and advocated an all-inclusive definition of folklore that accepted the productions of amateur choirs and theaters, materials of propaganda brigades, works by semiliterate authors, war songs, the material of so-called "industrial folklore," and other popular art forms.[18] Needless to say, the rest of the world did not adopt this broad definition of folklore.

In the thirties, adherents of the various schools of thought, such as the Finnish and formalist schools, terrified by the atmosphere of dread created by Stalin, began recanting their theories and confessing to "vulgar sociologism." It is difficult to assess the loss to the science of folkloristics caused by this climate of terror. Many folklorists changed their orientation. Vladimir Propp, as an example, no longer delved into the morphology and structure of the folktale. Instead, in *The Historical Roots of the Fairy Tale* (*Istoricheskie korni volshebnoi skazki*, 1946), he attempted to connect fairytale structure to initiation and funeral rites. On April 1, 1948, at Leningrad State University, A. G. Dement'ev accused Propp of basing his work on the works of foreign scholars, thereby robbing the Russian fairy tale of its national character. Accused of cosmopolitanism and depriving the Russian fairy tale of its national character, once again Propp was forced to recant or lose his teaching post at Leningrad State University, or face an even worse punishment. Indeed, the role of folklore was a nationalist one—to engender a patriotic love of the Mother Land and a deep respect for the working class.

The formalist school did not quite disappear. It produced disciples, a younger generation of folklorists who created the structural-semiotic school of folklore. Like the formalists, they explore the structure and semiotics of texts. The most important figure among them is Eleazar Meletinskii, who developed a methodology that expanded Propp's consideration of form to create a model of the folktale that included context.[19] Other members of this school include S. Nekliudov, D. Segal, and E. Novik. This group gained respect internationally. They have survived Soviet repression to prosper.

In addition, the collecting of folklore flourished in Soviet times and was encouraged by the government. Collectors continued to make contributions to the archives of the Russian Geographical Society, Moscow State University, the Academy of Arts and Sciences, and other repositories of folklore. In the thirties, M. K. Azadovskii collected tales in Siberia, and I. V. Karnaukhova collected northern tales and legends. Particularly noteworthy are collections of the repertoires of individual tellers, such as F. P. Gospodarev, I. F. Kovalev, M. M. Korguev, A. N. Korol'kova, N. O. Vinokurova, and others.

Despite the challenging climate, expeditions to collect folklore (especially in the Far North, Siberia, and Volga River areas), classification of materials collected, and the depositing of these materials in archives continued. After the Soviet Union fell, the republication of out-of-print works began. More importantly, the publication of previously forbidden genres, which had lain for years in archives (including personal archives), began. Collections of political jokes, indecent anecdotes, erotic folklore, and memorates (*bylichki*) began appearing on the shelves of bookstores and in the kiosks beside the subway entrances and on the city streets.

It is an exciting time to study Russian folklore. After the Soviet years of stagnation, a rebirth has occurred, and new knowledge is available.

Tellers and Tales

The folktale is an account of magical happenings and the wonderful adventures of heroes and heroines who, after many tests and battles, are rewarded for their courage and goodness. Goodness always wins over evil. A blend of fantasy and reality, the folktale is a source of popular wisdom, optimism, creativity, and poetry, handed down initially by word of mouth and later in written form.

In Russia, stories were recounted by soldiers, craftsmen, exiled prisoners, wandering pilgrims, loggers, and the like, for the entertainment of the folk. In return for food and a night's lodging, soldiers used to tell tales like "The Enchanted Princess," in which the soldier-hero accomplishes impressive deeds and earns the hand of the beautiful princess. At the end of a hard day's work, loggers used to gather around the fire and tell tales to while away the evening hours. Fishing artels frequently invited storytellers to accompany them on fishing expeditions and entertain them with stories. In ways such as these, rural life promoted the development of the folktale genre. Storytellers offered hardworking people whose existence was difficult a brief escape from reality.

The storyteller was always a welcome guest whose performance was like a theatrical presentation. The teller might change his or her voice to depict a specific story character, or gesticulate and act out a part. As a result, there was an emphasis on dialog with bare description, for storytellers relied upon gestures and props, instead of description, to demonstrate their point.

In later years, after the tales had been recorded, writers filled in the bare sections with descriptions of their own so that children and the general public, who were without the benefit of observing the teller, might enjoy the tales, too. As stories passed from performance to written text, the requirements for the creation of well-told stories changed along with the medium.

Several devices are used in the telling of tales, whether oral or written. Folktales may begin or end with formulas. For example, the story "The Fool and the Birch Tree" ends with the following couplet:

Regale me with ale

For telling my tale.

This verse is a reference to the custom of rewarding the storyteller with drink and food. Epithets are also commonly found in folktales. For example, Emelia, hero of "At the Pike's Command," is referred to as Emelia the Fool. The sea is referred to as "the blue sea." Terms of endearment are often used. For example, the tsarevna who loves Emelia refers to him as Emiliushka, the diminutive and endearing form of his name. Poetry may interrupt the story, as it does in "*Kolobok*, the Runaway Bun" and "The Silver Saucer and the Red Apple." These devices render color and rhythm to the stories.

Folktales have served as the basis of the works of writers like Aleksandr Pushkin, who used folklore motifs in his long poem "Ruslan and Liudmila." Nikolai Gogol incorporated Ukrainian folklore into his *Evenings on a Farm Near Dikanka*. Aleksandr Ostrovskii's dramatic tale *The Snow Maiden* and Pavel Bazhov's stories based on the folklore of the Ural Mountains represent just a few examples of writers influenced by this genre. Folktales have inspired the writers and readers of Russia alike, and undoubtedly they will continue to inspire future generations.

Classification of Folktales

Russian folklorists divide folktales into three types—animal tales (*skazki o zhivot-nykh*), fairy or magic tales (*volshebnye skazki*), and tales of everyday life (*bytovye skazki*).[20] This division is convenient and has been used here.

As mentioned previously, Stith Thompson in the United States and N. P. Andreev in Russia constructed tale type indexes based upon that of Antii Aarne. In some cases, tales may consist of more than one tale type. In other cases, there is a discrepancy between Thompson's and Andreev's descriptions of the same type. "Cheeky the Goat," for example, is Type 212 in both indexes. However, Thompson names Type 212 "The Lying Goat" and describes a goat that declares it has had nothing to eat when taken to pasture. Andreev names Type 212 "The Fleeced Goat" and describes a goat that steals a rabbit's home and is ousted with the help of other animals. The version chosen is true to both descriptions, but any single description is inadequate. "The Bubble, the Straw, and the *Lapot'*" (story Type 295) is categorized by both Andreev and Thompson as an animal tale, apparently because its structure is similar to that of an animal tale. However, since not a single animal appears in the tale, its classification flies in the face of logic. Here, the tale entitled "The Bubble, the Straw, and the *Lapot'*" has been placed under "Tales of Everyday Life" because the character-objects are common to peasant daily life. In short, no system is perfect, and I alone am responsible for category placement in this volume.

Animal Tales

Animal tales represent an ancient genre. They reflect concepts of animism, totemism, and anthropomorphism, tempered by satire and humor. Animals are known for specific traits. For example, the fox is sly and persuasive. In "Governor Kotofei Ivanovich, the Dreadful Cat," Elizaveta the Fox uses her cunning to elevate her cat husband above the other animals and to instill fear in them. The fox of "*Kolobok*, the Runaway Bun" charms and tricks the bun in a tale reminiscent of "The Gingerbread Boy." The goat is known for its stubbornness. Cheeky the Goat in the story of the same name sticks so stubbornly to her lies that she is found out and punished. The rabbit is cowardly. In the story entitled "Tails," the rabbit's cowardice prevents his leaving his hole to select a tail. The wolf is depicted as being slow-witted, and he usually receives a beating for his simplicity, as does the antihero-wolf of "The Wolf and the Old Man's Daughters." The bear is clumsy and not very clever. The bear often ends up inadvertently destroying something, as he does in "The Mansion-House" when he sits on the jug and crushes it. The antics of the animals in these stories model proper and improper behavior.

Fairy Tales

The fairy tale is more complex than the animal tale and involves several episodes. Frequently, the hero or heroine sets out on a journey, during which he or she is tested many times or has to do battle with an enemy, such as the wicked stepmother in "Father Frost" or the cannibalistic monster in "The Puff Monster." In the Russian Cinderella tale entitled "Pigskin," it is the stepfather who is the villain.

Baba Yaga is a central figure in Russian folklore. She appears in the fairy tale as a frightful figure living in the forest in a hut on chicken legs, which is located between the kingdom of the living and the dead. She is a nature spirit who flies through the air in a mortar, which she steers with a pestle while sweeping away her tracks with a broom. She may be good or evil in accordance with her mood, so she alternates between helper and villain in relation to the hero. She appears in the story "Teryoshechka" in her evil guise, imitating the voice of Teryoshechka's mother to lure the boy into her clutches.

Assisted by innate goodness and by human or animal helpers, the hero or heroine defeats evil and is transformed by misfortune into a wiser adult who experiences the predictable happy ending. Thus, Teryoshechka defeats Baba Yaga and returns matured to his parents. The heroic soldier of "The Enchanted Princess" receives a bride as a reward for his bravery in freeing the princess from a magic spell. Alyonushka of "The Silver Saucer and the Red Apple" is rescued from a cruel death inflicted by her sisters when a kind woman gives her father a flask containing the water of life. Alyonushka confronts the issue of sibling rivalry and emerges victorious. Goodness prevails, but for those who are not good and behave badly, the fairytale ending is quite different. Thus, the loutish stepsister of the tale entitled "Father Frost" pays with her life for her surliness.

Tales of Everyday Life

Russian folklorists often place the word "social" (*sotsial'no*) before the designation "tales of everyday life," thereby emphasizing the social satire aspect of the genre. Tales of everyday life evolved more recently than animal or fairy tales and are closer to reality. Lives of common people are depicted, and the characters are less exotic than those who inhabit the fairy tale. The heroes are peasants, priests, and soldiers—familiar, everyday people. The situation these characters face is frequently humorous and their approach to solving predicaments absurd. For example, the peasant couple and the priest's family in "The Egg" react to the accidental breaking of an egg as if it were a grave tragedy. In the story entitled "Magic Water," the old woman actually believes that the quarrels with her husband have stopped because of the magical properties of the water she is holding in her mouth, rather than because she is keeping her mouth shut. The wily common man is frequently the hero of tales of everyday life. Thus, the soldier of "A Copeck a Drop" who outwits his miserly hostess so that he can have oil in his soup is an example. So, too, is the con man of "The Sorcerer," who is able to solve the case of the disappearance of the tsar's ring with cunning and luck.

Tales of Spirits and the Supernatural

Tales of spirits and the supernatural are known as *bylichki*, and they constitute a unique genre. In the Soviet era, the study of this genre was discouraged. American folklorists call these stories memorates. They are related by the person who actually experienced the event or are told as having happened to a friend or family member of the teller. The narrator tells of his or her encounter with a supernatural being, such as a werewolf, house spirit (*domovoi*), mermaid, wood goblin (*leshii*), or the like. These creatures are nature spirits who are part of the Russian pagan belief system. The wood goblin (*leshii*) is the master of the forest. He has a bad habit of frightening people with his evil laugh and leading them astray. In "The Wood Goblin Godfather," however, the little wood goblin protects a small child. The house spirit (*domovoi*) guards the family and livestock of the house in which he lives. In the past, when a peasant family moved, a member of the household scooped up ashes from the hearth and transported the house spirit, who was believed to be in the ashes, to the new domicile. The family believed that if it failed to do so, it would have bad luck. The spirit of the bathhouse (*bannik*) is especially evil and vicious. He lives in the bathhouse, which is associated with rituals attending birth and death, waiting for an unsuspecting soul to break one of the bathhouse rules so that he can smother and skin alive the transgressor.

About Tale Selection and Translation

In selecting the stories, I searched for ones that were told by talented tellers. In so doing, I turned mostly to retellings and literary renditions by Russian writers, rather than to authentic recordings from the mouths of the folk. I made my selections from well-known collections and retellings, which have appealed over the ages to Russian children, parents, teachers, and librarians, as well as to my students and storytelling audiences. In a few instances, I have added flourishes of my own if elaboration or explanation was required. It is well known that the greatest of Russian tale collectors, Aleksandr Afanas'ev, doctored bare tellings to some extent, so there is a precedent for what I have done. Afanas'ev is just one of the collectors and taletellers upon whose work my renditions are based. Others include Aleksei N. Tolstoi, Èrna V. Pomerantseva, and Vladimir P. Anikin. The latter two are well-known Russian folklorists. Chair of the Department of Folklore at Moscow State University after Nikolai I. Kravtsov retired, Vladimir P. Anikin was my teacher and Russian dissertation adviser.

There are many splendid collections of Russian folktales in English. They include those of Aleksandr Nikolaevich Afanas'ev, Arthur Ransome, Jeremiah Curtin, Virginia Haviland, William Ralston, and James Riordan, to name a few. It would be difficult indeed to improve on their work. My intent is to complement these collections with contextual information about Russia's history, geography, and cultural traditions, and to introduce the reader to commonly beloved folktales that have appeared in school readers for decades. Thus, every Russian child is familiar with "*Kolobok*, the Runaway Bun," "The Mansion-House," "Father Frost," "At the Pike's Command," "The Egg," and many other tales represented here. Although most of the stories selected are well known in Russia and have been published there over and over again, some innovative additions have been made, such as the tale entitled "The Puff Monster," which was told by twelve-year-old Aleksandra Pozniakova. To my knowledge, tales of spirits and the supernatural (*bylichki*) have never appeared before in an English collection, although translations have appeared in some scholarly works, such as Linda J. Ivanits' *Russian Folk Belief.*

Although with some exceptions I have used the Library of Congress System of Transliteration, no attempt was made to unify or standardize spellings from various English sources to fit within that scheme. Some spellings have been modified from that system to facilitate pronunciation. The photographs are my own. They were taken from 1989 to 2001.

The world of the Russian folktale is a fascinating one. No one can venture into this domain without being richly rewarded in enjoyment and in the acquisition of knowledge. Long after the book has been closed, the reader will remember the brave and clever heroes and heroines who faced the unknown and conquered both their fears and the enemy.

Notes

1. *World Almanac and Book of Facts 2003*, s.v. "Russia: Russian Federation."

2. Nicholas V. Riasanovsky, *A History of Russia*, 4th ed. (New York and Oxford: Oxford University Press, 1984), 18–19.

3. For selected tales from the *Primary Chronicle*, see Serge A. Zenkovsky, ed. and trans., "Stories from the *Primary Chronicle*," *Medieval Russia's Epics, Chronicles, and Tales* (1963; rev. ed., New York: Dutton, 1974), 43–77.

4. Sidney Harcave, *Russia: A History*, 4th ed. (Chicago: Lippincott, 1959), 45.

5. Ibid, 103.

6. For an explanation of this viewpoint, see Erla Zwingle, "Catherine the Great," *National Geographic* 194, no. 3 (September 1998): 92–117.

7. For a description of Napoleon's invasion, see Harcave, *Russia: A History*, 193–197 and Riasanovsky, *A History of Russia*, 310–314.

8. Riazanovsky, *A History of Russia*, 312.

9. Anecdotes have been selected from author's field collections.

10. Lenin hatched many of his revolutionary ideas in Switzerland. He rode in a sealed train car from Switzerland to Russia to carry out the Russian Revolution of 1917.

11. For Russia's space landmarks, see Riazanovsky, *A History of Russia*, 582.

12. *World Almanac 2003*, s.v. "Russia: Russian Federation."

13. Jim Heintz, "Moscow Counts the Dead after Standoff Ends," *Manchester Union Leader/New Hampshire Sunday News*, October 27, 2002: A5.

14. "Russia," *The World Factbook 2002*, Available: http://www.cia.gov/cia/publications/factbook/geos/rs.html (accessed May 16, 2003).

15. *World Almanac 2003*, s.v. "Russia: Russian Federation." Twenty million Russians receive the equivalent of $31 a month, and most pensioners receive less than $100 a month (Fen Montaigne, "Russia Rising," *National Geographic* 200, no. 5 [November 2001]: 9, 21).

16. For a history of Russian folklore, consult Y. M. Sokolov, *Russian Folklore*, trans. Catherine Ruth Smith, with introduction and bibliography by Felliz J. Oinas (Detroit: Folklore Associates, 1971), 40–155.

17. V. Ia. Propp, *Morfologiia skazki*, 2nd ed., Issledovaniia po fol'kloru i mifologii vostoka (1928; reprint, Moscow: Nauka, 1969), 103.

18. See K. V. Chistov's article "Folkloristics and the Present Day," in *The Study of Russian Folklore*, eds. Felix Oinas and Stephen Soudakoff, Indiana University Folklore Institute Monograph Series, vol. 25 (The Hague and Paris: Mouton, 1975), 303–317.

19. E. M. Meletinskii, S. Iu. Nekliudov, E. S. Novik, and D. M. Segal, "Eshche raz o probleme strukturnogo opisaniia volshebnoi skazki," *Trudy po znakovym sistemam* 5 (1971): 63–91.

20. These classifications are used in all monographs about the folktale. For details, see Vladimir P. Anikin, *Russkaia narodnaia skazka: Posobie dlia uchitelei* (Moscow: Prosveshchenie, 1977).

Additional Sources Consulted

Books and Articles

Aarne, Antii. *The Types of the Folktale: A Classification and Bibliography.* Trans. and enlarged by Stith Thompson. 2nd ed. FF Communications 184. Helsinki: Suomalainen Tiedeakatemia Academia Scientiarum Fennica, 1961.

Andreev, N. P. *Ukazatel' skazochnikh siuzhetov po sisteme Aarne.* 1929. Reprint, Berkeley: Berkeley Slavic Specialties, 1993.

Anikin, V. P. *Russkoe ustnoe narodnoe tvorchestvo (fol'klor): Metodicheskie ukazaniia.* Moscow: Izdatel'stvo MGU, 1981.

Cultural Handbook to the New Independent States. Washington, DC: ACTR/ACCELS, 1995.

Gerhart, Genevra. *The Russian's World: Life and Language.* New York: Holt, Rinehart and Winston, 1974; New York: Harcourt Brace, 1995; Bloomington, IN: Slavica, 2001.

Goldman, Minton F. *Russia, the Eurasian Republics, and Central/Eastern Europe.* 7th ed. Global Studies. Guilford, CT: Dushkin/McGraw-Hill, 1999.

Haney, Jack V. *An Introduction to the Russian Folktale.* The Complete Russian Folktale, vol. 1. Armonk, NY: M.E. Sharpe, 1999.

Ivanits, Linda J. *Russian Folk Belief.* Armonk, NY: M.E. Sharpe, 1989.

Kravtsov, N. I., ed. *Russkoe narodnoe poèticheskoe tvorchestvo: Uchebnoe posobie dlia filologicheskikh fakul'tetov pedagogicheskikh institutov.* Moscow: Prosveshchenie, 1971.

Kravtsov, N. I., and A. V. Kulagina. *Programma kursa 'Slavianskii fol'klor dlia filologicheskikh fakul'tetov gosudarstvennykh universitetov.* Moscow: Izdatel'stvo MGU, 1978.

Kulagina, A. V. *Russkoe ustnoe narodnoe tvorchestvo: Programma kursa i metodicheskoe posobie.* 2nd ed. Moscow: Izdatel'stvo Universiteta rossiiskoi akademii obrazovaniia, 1997.

Novikov, N. V. *Obrazy vostochnoslavianskoi volshebnoi skazki.* Leningrad: Nauka, 1974.

Petrukhin, V. Ia., T. A. Agapkina, L. N. Vinogradova, and S. M. Tolstaia, eds. *Slavianskaia mifologiia: Èntsiklopedicheskii slovar'.* Moscow: Ellis lak, 1995.

Maps

Fetisova, N. P., ed. *Geograficheskii atlas SSSR dlia 7-go klassa.* Cartographers Z. F. Antonova, D. I. Zhiv, L. N. Kolosova, and V. D. Semenova. Rev. ed. Moscow: Glavnoe upravlenie geodesii i kartografii pri Sovete ministrov SSSR, 1975.

Gilbert, Martin. *Atlas of Russian History.* 1972. Reprint, New York: Dorset Press, 1985.

Okatova, A. L., ed. *Russkaia Federatsiia.* Cartographers I. S. Ushakova, M. I. Kolomeichenko, and L. S. Belikova. Nazran', Republic of Ingushetiia: AST, 2000.

PART 1

ANIMAL TALES

KOLOBOK, THE RUNAWAY BUN

Once upon a time, there lived an old woman and an old man. One day the old man said to the old woman, "Go to the grain bin and see if you can scrape together enough flour to make a bun."

The old woman swept out the grain bin with a hen's wing and managed to scrape together two handfuls of flour. She mixed the flour with sour cream and made a bun. Then, she fried the bun in oil and put it on the window sill to cool.

Kolobok, the little bun, lay there so long that it got bored. Then, it began to roll— from the window sill to the bench, from the bench to the floor, and from the floor to the door. It jumped across the threshold and into the hall. It rolled from the hall to the porch, from the porch into the yard, from the yard to the gate, farther and farther away.

The little bun rolled along the road until it came upon a rabbit. The rabbit said, "Little bun, little bun, I am going to eat you up!"

Kolobok, the runaway bun, answered, "If you promise not to eat me up, Mr. Rabbit, I will sing you a little song.

I am a runaway bun.
I was scraped from a grain bin
And mixed with sour cream
And fried in oil
And cooled on a window sill.
I ran away from an old woman
And a little old man,
And I can run away from you
Even more easily, I can!

Then, the runaway bun rolled down the road while the rabbit looked on helplessly.

Kolobok, the bun, rolled on until it met a wolf. The wolf said, "Little bun, little bun, I am going to eat you up!"

The runaway bun answered, "If you promise not to eat me up, Mr. Wolf, I will sing you a little song.

I am a runaway bun.

I was scraped from a grain bin

And mixed with sour cream

And fried in oil

And cooled on a window sill.

I ran away from an old woman

And a little old man

And a rabbit,

And I can run away from you

Even more easily, I can!"

And the runaway bun began rolling down the road again while the wolf looked on in bewilderment.

Kolobok, the bun, rolled along the road and came upon a bear. The bear said, "Little bun, little bun, I am going to eat you up!"

The runaway bun answered, "Indeed? You think you can eat me up, you clumsy oaf?

I am a runaway bun.

I was scraped from a grain bin

And mixed with sour cream

And fried in oil

And cooled on a window sill.

I ran away from an old woman

And a little old man

And a rabbit

And a wolf,

And I can run away from you

Even more easily, I can!"

And the runaway bun began rolling again while the bear looked on and scratched his head.

Kolobok, the bun, rolled on until it met a fox. The fox said, "Little bun, little bun, where are you rolling?"

The runaway bun answered, "I am rolling down the road."

The fox said, "Little bun, little bun, sing me a song."

Kolobok, the bun, sang:

"I am a runaway bun.

I was scraped from a grain bin
And mixed with sour cream
And fried in oil
And cooled on a window sill.
I ran away from an old woman
And a little old man
And a rabbit
And a wolf
And a bear,
And it will be easy for me
To run away from here!"

The fox said, "Oh, what a pretty song! But I can't hear it very well. Little bun, little bun, sit on my nose and sing it again, a little louder this time, please."

Kolobok, the runaway bun, jumped up on the fox's nose and sang its song in a louder voice.

The fox pretended that she could not hear. She said to *Kolobok*, "Little bun, little bun, sit on my tongue and try singing just once more."

Kolobok, the runaway bun, jumped onto the fox's tongue and—snap! The fox ate the runaway bun all up.

THE MANSION-HOUSE

A peasant was riding along with a cartload of crockery when one of the jugs fell from the top of the cart and rolled to the side of the road. The peasant, not noticing that he had lost one of his wares, traveled on.

Sorrowful the Fly was flying by, and she caught sight of the jug. "Whose mansion-house is this?" she asked. "Who lives here?"

No one answered. There was no one at home, so Sorrowful the Fly flew into the jug and set up housekeeping.

The next day Whiner the Mosquito flew up to the jug and asked, "Whose mansion-house is this? Who lives here?"

"I do, Sorrowful the Fly. And who are you?"

"I am Whiner the Mosquito."

"Why not come in and live with me?" asked Sorrowful the Fly.

Whiner the Mosquito accepted the invitation gladly, and the two insects began living together in peace and harmony.

Nibbles the Mouse was taking a stroll when she spied the jug. "Whose mansion-house is this?" she asked. "Who lives here?"

A tiny voice answered, "We do, Sorrowful the Fly and Whiner the Mosquito. And who are you?"

"I am Nibbles the Mouse."

"Come live with us, Nibbles."

Nibbles the Mouse went inside, and all three creatures began living together.

The next day Croaker the Frog came hopping up to the mansion-house. She asked, "Whose mansion-house is this? Who lives here?"

"I do, Sorrowful the Fly."

"I do, Whiner the Mosquito."

"And I do, Nibbles the Mouse. And who are you?"

"I am Croaker the Frog."

"Do come live with us, Croaker," said the inhabitants of the jug.

The frog hopped into the jug happily, and the four of them began living together.

Soon afterwards Skipper the Rabbit hopped past the jug. He caught sight of it and asked, "Whose mansion-house is this? Who lives here?"

"I do, Sorrowful the Fly."

"I do, Whiner the Mosquito."

"I do, Nibbles the Mouse."

"I do, Croaker the Frog. And who are you?"

"I am Skipper the Rabbit."

"Come join us, friend!" said the inhabitants of the jug.

The rabbit skipped into the jug, and all five friends began living together.

Soon, along came Sister Fox. She knocked on the side of the jug and asked, "Whose mansion-house is this? Who lives here?"

"I do, Sorrowful the Fly."

"I do, Whiner the Mosquito."

"I do, Nibbles the Mouse."

"I do, Croaker the Frog."

"I do, Skipper the Rabbit. And who are you?"

"I am silver-tongued Sister Fox."

"Come live with us, Sister Fox," said the inhabitants of the jug.

The fox climbed into the jug, and all six friends began living happily together.

That night Gray-legs the Wolf came by. He looked into the opening of the jug and asked, "Whose mansion-house is this? Who lives here?"

"I do, Sorrowful the Fly."

"I do, Whiner the Mosquito."

"I do, Nibbles the Mouse."

"I do, Croaker the Frog."

"I do, Skipper the Rabbit."

"I do, Sister Fox. And who are you?"

"I am Gray-legs the Wolf."

"Well, come live with us, Gray-legs!"

The wolf climbed into the jug. Although it was becoming a little crowded to say the least, all seven friends began living together in happiness and harmony. They sang songs and made merry all day long.

One day Fumble Paws the Bear heard singing coming from the jug. He stopped short and roared with all his might, "Whose mansion-house is this? Who lives here?"

"I do, Sorrowful the Fly."

"I do, Whiner the Mosquito."

"I do, Nibbles the Mouse."

"I do, Croaker the Frog."

"I do, Skipper the Rabbit."

"I do, Sister Fox."

"I do, Gray-legs the Wolf. And who are you?"

"I am Fumble Paws the Bear."

"Come live with us, Fumble Paws."

"Why, thank you," said the bear. He tried to crawl into the jug. He pushed, and he pushed. He snorted and groaned, but he could not squeeze into the jug.

"I had better sit on top of the jug," he decided.

Fumble Paws the Bear climbed onto the top of the jug. No sooner did he sit down than smash—he squashed the jug to pieces!

As the jug was falling apart, there was barely enough time for Sorrowful the Fly, Whiner the Mosquito, Nibbles the Mouse, Croaker the Frog, Skipper the Rabbit, Sister Fox, and Gray-legs the Wolf to escape unharmed. All of the creatures living in the jug ran off to the forest, where they searched for a new home.

TAILS

A rumor circulated in the forest that tails would be given out to every creature. The talkative magpies flew to every corner of the forests, glades, and meadows, and announced to creatures great and small, "Come to the big glade tomorrow to receive your tail."

The animals and the birds became excited. "Tails? What tails? Why tails?"

"Whatever they may be, we should take them since they are being given away," said Sister Fox. "We'll figure out what they are for later."

Beginning early in the morning, a line of creatures stretched to the big glade. Some came running, others came hopping, and still others came flying. All of them wanted to receive a tail.

A little rabbit wanted to go, too. He poked his head out of his hole. He saw that a hard rain was falling, so hard that it whipped his snout.

The rabbit got scared. "The rain will beat me and hurt me," he said, and he hid deep in his rabbit hole.

While he was sitting there, he heard "stomp, stomp, stomp." The earth was shaking, and the trees and bushes were creaking and crackling. A bear was passing by.

The rabbit poked his snout out of the hole. "Grandfather Bear, when they give out tails, grab a tail for me, please," said the rabbit.

"All right," the bear said, "if I don't forget, I'll grab one for you."

The bear left, and the little rabbit grew thoughtful. "The bear is old. He'll forget about me. I'd better ask someone else."

Suddenly, he heard "trip, trip, trip." A wolf was passing by.

The rabbit poked out his snout and said, "Uncle Wolf, when you receive your tail, pick out one for me, please."

"All right," said the wolf, "I'll bring one if there are any left." And he ran off.

The rabbit sat in his hole listening to the grass rustling and swaying. Suddenly, a fox came running. "I should ask the fox to bring me a tail," thought the rabbit.

"Sister Fox, when you are receiving your new tail, bring a tail for me, please," said the rabbit.

"All right," said the fox, "I'll bring you a tail." Then, the fox ran off.

Many creatures went to the glade where tails were hanging from tree branches. There were tails of every type—fluffy ones and others in the shape of fans or brooms, smooth ones and others in the shape of a stick or a pretzel or a curl, long and short ones—in short, there were all kinds of tails.

The fox was the first to arrive. She chose a fluffy, soft tail. She went home very pleased with her choice. She twisted her tail around, admiring it.

The horse ran up and chose a tail with long hair. What a tail it was! He had only to flap it, and it extended to his ears. It would serve him well to drive away flies. The horse left quite satisfied indeed.

The cow approached. She selected a tail that was long, like a stick, with a broom on the end. The cow was happy. She waved her tail along her sides to drive away the insects that clung to her.

The pig approached. She could not raise her head very high, so she had to take the tail that hung the lowest. It was smooth, like a rope. She did not like it at first. But she twisted it into a ring. How beautiful it seemed then! She decided that it was the best of all tails.

The elephant came tramping and tromping. He had damaged his feet by tramping too much. Only one tail remained. It was like a cord with a bristle on the end. The elephant did not like it, but there was nothing he could do. He had no other choice.

The bear was late because on the way he had come upon a beehive. When he arrived, there were no tails left. He found a piece of hide with fur on it. He took the hide and wore it like a tail. It was good that it was black, the same color as his fur.

After they had selected their tails, the animals went home.

The rabbit sat in his hole waiting anxiously for someone to bring him a tail. He heard the bear approach. "Grandfather bear, did you bring me a tail?" he asked.

"How could I bring you a tail? I barely managed to grab a scrap of tail for myself," said the bear. Then, he left.

The rabbit heard the wolf running by. "Uncle wolf, did you bring me a tail?" asked the rabbit.

"I wasn't thinking of you, squint eyes. I hardly managed to select a thick, fluffy tail for myself," said the wolf, and he ran away.

The fox came running. "Sister Fox, did you bring me a tail?" asked the rabbit.

"Oh, I forgot," said the fox. "But see what a magnificent tail I selected for myself!" The fox began twirling her tail in every direction. The rabbit was offended. He almost burst into tears.

Suddenly, the rabbit heard a noise, the sound of hissing and barking. The cat and dog were fighting about whose tail was better. They quarreled and quarreled and fought until the dog had gnawed off the end of the cat's tail.

The rabbit grabbed the scrap of cat's tail and stuck it onto his backside. The rabbit was very pleased with the result. It was a small tail, but it was a tail all the same.

THE ROOSTER AND THE HEN

Once upon a time there lived an old woman and an old man. They had a rooster and a hen. The rooster and the hen liked to go to the forest to pick nuts.

One day the rooster and hen begged, "Granny, please let us go to the forest to pick nuts."

"Go ahead," the old woman said.

So the rooster and the hen walked to the forest. They walked on and on until they came upon a big, leafy hazelnut tree.

"Fly up into the hazelnut tree," the rooster said to the hen.

"No, I won't, rooster. Fly up into the tree yourself."

The rooster flew—flap, flap—into the air. He flew onto a tree limb. There he sat cracking nuts.

"Oh, rooster, throw some nuts down to me," said the hen.

The rooster threw down a nut, but he did not throw it far enough. He threw another nut, but it fell too far away. He threw a third nut, and it hit the hen in the eye. The hen sat by the forest path crying.

An old man came walking down the path. When he saw the hen crying, he asked, "Little hen, why are you crying?"

"Why wouldn't I cry?" said the hen. "The rooster has poked out my eye."

The old man went to the rooster. "Rooster, why did you poke out the hen's eye?"

"I poked out the hen's eye because the hazelnut tree tore my trousers and caused me to aim badly," said the rooster.

The old man addressed the hazelnut tree. "Hazelnut tree, why did you tear the rooster's trousers?"

"I tore the rooster's trousers because some goats came by and picked my leaves, making my branches bare and sharp so that they tore the rooster's trousers."

The old man went after the goats, who were running from tree to tree gleaning a leafy feast. "Goats, why did you pick the leaves off the hazelnut tree?"

"We picked the leaves off the hazelnut tree because the shepherd didn't take us to pasture."

The old man went to the shepherd. "Shepherd, why didn't you take the goats to pasture?"

"My wife didn't give me any pancakes to eat, so I didn't have the strength to take the goats to pasture," the shepherd replied.

The old man went to the shepherd's wife. "Oh, shepherd's wife, why didn't you make pancakes for your husband?"

"I didn't make pancakes because the pig turned over the bowl of pancake dough and spilled it onto the ground," said the shepherd's wife.

The old man went into the yard and walked up to the pigpen. "Pig, why did you spill the mistress's pancake dough?"

"I knocked over the pancake dough while I was chasing the wolf, who carried away my piglet."

The old man walked down the road until he met up with the wolf. "Wolf, why did you carry off the pig's piglet?" he asked.

"I carried off the piglet because I was hungry. I wanted to eat," the wolf replied. The wolf was the only one who did not attempt to justify or rationalize his behavior.

VASKA THE CAT

Once upon a time a cat, a goat, and a ram lived in the barnyard. They lived together in friendship. If they had a wisp of hay, they always divided it equally.

If one of them occasionally got a pitchfork poked into his side, it was always Vaska the Cat. He was a terrible thief and bandit. He was on the hunt every moment, poking his nose where it did not belong.

One day the goat and the ram were lolling about talking. Suddenly, they spied the gray forehead of the purring Vaska. The cat approached, whining pitifully.

"Oh, Vaska, kitty cat with the gray forehead, why are you crying? Why are you hopping on three legs?" asked the goat and the ram.

"Why wouldn't I cry?" replied the cat. "The old woman beat me and pulled my ears. She hurt my leg and squeezed me as if she were a boa constrictor."

"Why did such a misfortune befall you?" asked the goat and the ram.

"The old woman was mean to me because I accidentally licked up the sour cream," whined the cat. Again, he burst into tears.

"Vaska, kitty cat with the gray forehead, what else are you crying about?"

"How could I not cry? The old woman beat me and said, 'Now where will I get sour cream when my son-in-law comes to visit? Instead of serving him sour cream, I'll have to slaughter the goat and the ram and serve them for dinner.'"

After hearing these words, the goat and the ram set up a fearful howl. "Oh, you slow-witted gray cat, you are the ruin of us."

The three animals began thinking about what they could do. All three of them decided to run away.

"Brother Ram, is your forehead strong?" asked the cat. "Try pushing open the gate."

The ram took a flying leap and butted the gate with his forehead. The gate shook, but it did not open.

Then, Brother Goat had a go at it. He took a flying leap, butted the gate, and the gate flew open.

Away ran the goat and the ram. A column of dust rose into the air. The grass was trampled to the ground. Vaska, the gray cat, followed them, hopping along on three legs.

Soon, the cat grew tired. "Brother Ram and Brother Goat, don't leave your little brother to be eaten by wild beasts," Vaska begged.

The goat put the cat on his back. They rushed over hills and down dales and across quicksand. They ran day and night until they had no strength at all left in their legs.

Finally, they came to a mown field. Stacks of hay were standing in the field. The goat and the ram stopped to rest.

The night was cold. "Where can we get a fire?" thought the goat and the ram.

The purring Vaska already had gathered some birch bark. He turned the goat's horns so that they were facing the ram's horns and ordered the goat and the ram to bump foreheads.

The goat and the ram hit foreheads so hard that they created sparks. The cat used the sparks to set the birch bark afire.

"Good," said Vaska, the gray cat. "Now, we'll get warm." He set a stack of hay on fire.

The three friends gathered around the fire. They barely had gotten warm when they looked around and saw an uninvited guest approaching—Mikhailo Ivanovich, the bear.

"Let me get warm and rest a bit, brothers," said the bear. "I don't feel well."

"Welcome, Mikhailo Ivanovich. Where have you come from?"

"I went to the beehives in search of honey. But I got into a fight with some men there. That's why I'm sick. I'm on my way to the fox to be doctored."

The four animals began whiling away the night. The bear settled beneath the haystack. The purring cat climbed to the top of the haystack. The goat and the ram chose a place by the fire.

Soon the bear, the goat, and the ram were asleep. While they were dozing, the purring cat alone did not sleep. Instead, he kept watch. Suddenly, he noticed seven gray wolves and one white wolf approaching. The wolves were headed right for the fire.

"Aha, what kind of folks do we have here?" the white wolf asked the goat and the ram. "Let's fight! We'll see who's stronger!"

The goat and the ram began bleating, but Vaska said, "Hey, there, white wolf, you must be the head wolf. Don't anger our chief. He has a vile temper. When he flies off the handle, it's bad for everyone. Can't you see his beard? That's where his strength lies. He kills wild animals with his beard and uses his horns to skin them. You would do well to approach him with respect. Ask him if you might play with his younger brother, who is lying beneath the haystack."

The wolves bowed to the goat. Then, they surrounded Mikhailo the Bear and began playing with him.

The bear had rested long enough to get his strength back. He struck a wolf with his paw. The wolf began howling. Then, his brother wolves began howling, too. They put their tails between their legs and ran away as fast as they could.

The goat and the ram grabbed Vaska the Cat. The goat put him on his back, and they ran home at top speed.

"We've had enough of wandering around aimlessly," they said. "We have no need of misfortunes and misadventures."

When the animals arrived home, the old woman and the old man were very happy indeed to see them. Thereafter, Brother Goat, Brother Ram, and Vaska the Cat stayed home. They never ran away again.

THE WOLF AND THE OLD MAN'S DAUGHTERS

One day an old man, who had three daughters, prepared to go to the field to plow. Before leaving, he said to his daughters, "I am going to the field to plow. I'm not taking my lunch with me. You girls bake some bread and make me a lunch. Then, bring the lunch to me."

"Where can we find you, Dad?" asked his oldest daughter.

"I'm going to the strip of field I began plowing yesterday. I'll throw wood shavings along the path that I take so that you can find me."

The old man set out, dropping wood shavings along the way.

A wolf came along and gathered up all the shavings. Carefully, the wolf put the shavings on the path that led to his lair.

The oldest daughter sent her youngest sister to the field. "Go take Dad his lunch," she said.

The youngest girl grabbed the lunch. "Sister, where can I find Father? Where should I take his lunch?"

"He has strewn wood shavings along the path that he took. Follow the wood shavings, and you will find him," said the oldest girl.

The youngest daughter set out down the path following the wood shavings. She came to the wolf's lair and went in.

Soon the wolf appeared. "My, oh my, the Lord has sent me a wife," he declared when he saw the girl.

The youngest daughter was afraid. She did not run away, but sat in the corner of the wolf's lair.

When the old man returned home that evening, he asked, "Why didn't you bring my lunch, daughters?"

The oldest daughter replied, "Our youngest sister left to bring your lunch to you, but she hasn't come home."

Sadly, the old man and his daughters went to sleep without the youngest girl.

In the morning the old man got out of bed and harnessed the horse. Before setting out for the field, he said, "My clever daughters, come to the field and bring me lunch. Today I'm going to do the harrowing. I'm going to level the soil in the field to prepare it for planting."

"Dad, please take us with you," his daughters begged.

"No, daughters, you must stay home to bake the bread," the old man replied.

"Very well, then, we'll bake the bread. Where can we find you?"

"When I went to the field yesterday, I threw wood shavings along the path I took. This time I'll make two rows of wood shavings, so that you will certainly find me."

As the old man walked along, he dropped two rows of wood shavings, side by side. The wolf came along and gathered up the shavings. Then, the wolf dropped the shavings along the path that led to his lair.

This time the middle daughter set out to bring her father his lunch. She followed the wood shavings to the wolf's lair, and there she found her younger sister.

Soon, the wolf came home. When he saw the old man's middle daughter, he said, "Aha, the Lord has given me two wives."

In the evening the old man prepared to go home. He had eaten neither lunch nor dinner. Believing that his daughters had forgotten him, he wept and sang sad songs.

When he arrived home, he said to his oldest daughter, "Oh, my dear daughter, my clever daughter, why didn't you bring my lunch? Why didn't you come to the field?"

"Why, Dad, yesterday I sent my youngest sister to you, and today I baked a pie and sent my middle sister to you. She set out with the pie, but she hasn't returned home."

"What a misfortune," the old man declared. "You sent your foolish sisters, instead of going yourself. This time I'll make three rows of wood shavings on the path to the field."

The next day the old man made three rows of wood shavings along the path, but once again the wolf gathered up the shavings and strewed them along the path leading to his lair.

This time the oldest daughter set out with her father's lunch. She found the wood shavings and followed them to the wolf's lair. She entered the lair and found her two sisters there.

When the wolf returned home, he said, "Aha, now I have three wives!" From that day on the wolf kept the three girls deep inside his lair.

One day the oldest sister said to the wolf, "Oh, husband, take this little present to Father. I've baked him a pie."

But the oldest sister had not baked a pie. Instead, she had tied her youngest sister in a sack and she placed the sack on the wolf's back.

"Take this gift to Father, gray wolf," she said.

The wolf grabbed the sack and set out carrying it. He had not gone very far when it seemed to him that the sack was rather heavy. "I'll just sit on this tree stump for a little while, and I'll have a piece of the pie," he said aloud.

The girl in the sack answered, "Don't sit on the tree stump, and don't eat the pie. Take Father his present."

"Ai, wife, how can you hear me?" asked the wolf.

The wolf continued on his way. He brought the sack to his father-in-law's yard. The dogs caught sight of him and ran after him. They grabbed hold of his pants with their teeth and ripped them off.

The wolf ran home. "Wife!" he cried.

"What do you want, gray wolf?" asked the oldest sister.

"My brothers-in-law invited me to visit," he said.

"Why didn't you spend the night with them?"

"I lost my trousers there," said the wolf.

The next morning the oldest sister said, "Gray wolf, take this gift to Father."

"Give it to me," said the wolf.

Once again the oldest sister had failed to bake a pie. Instead, she had placed her middle sister into the sack.

"Here, take this pie to Father," she ordered.

The wolf set out. This time the sack seemed even heavier. "I'll just sit on this tree stump for a while," he said, "and I'll eat a little piece of pie."

The girl in the sack said, "Don't sit on the tree stump. And don't eat the pie!"

"Ai, wife, how can you hear me?" asked the wolf.

The wolf came to his father-in-law's yard. He hopped over the fence. The dogs began tearing him to pieces. He barely escaped alive and arrived home trembling.

"Wife, my brothers-in-law invited me to visit, and they almost skinned me alive," said the wolf.

"Gray wolf, tomorrow take Father a present from me and spend the night with your brothers-in-law," said the oldest sister.

This time she got into the sack herself. The wolf grabbed the sack and dragged it to his father-in-law's.

When he arrived at his father-in-law's home, the dogs began tearing him to pieces. The wolf did not know where to run. The dogs chased him and tore him to shreds. They dragged him to the field and left him there.

The old man was delighted to have all of his daughters at home again, safe and sound. After their adventure, the father and his daughters lived a long and happy life.

GOVERNOR KOTOFEI IVANOVICH, THE DREADFUL CAT

A peasant once owned a cat. The cat was a scamp, and he gave the man a great deal of trouble. In fact, he pestered the life out of him. The peasant thought and thought about what he should do. Finally he grabbed the cat, put him into a sack, and took him to the forest. When he got to the forest, he threw the sack as far as he could, and it disappeared. The peasant returned home, happy to be rid of the cat once and for all.

Meanwhile, finding himself in a huge forest, the cat walked on and on until he came upon a little cottage. He climbed into the attic of the cottage and rested. Soon he grew hungry, so he returned to the forest to catch some mice and birds. When he had eaten his fill, he went back to the attic, not caring a bit about where he was or the fact that he was all alone in the world.

One day when the cat was taking a stroll, he met a fox named Elizaveta. The fox looked at the cat and marveled.

"I have lived a good many years in the forest, but never before have I seen an animal like you! Who are you, my good man? How did you happen to come here, and what is your name?"

The cat bristled and answered, "Just call me Governor Kotofei Ivanovich. I was sent from the Siberian forests to be governor of your province."

"Oh, Governor Kotofei," said Elizaveta, "I hadn't heard anything about your coming. Well, please do stay with me as my guest."

So the cat went with the fox. She led him to her den and treated him to various wild game and delicacies. Then, she asked him, "Kotofei Ivanovich, are you married, or are you a bachelor?"

"I am a bachelor."

"I am unmarried myself. Why don't you ask me to be your wife?"

The cat agreed, and they began to celebrate their marriage with feasting and merry-making.

The next day, Elizaveta went out to get something to eat while the cat stayed home. She caught a duck and was carrying it back to her den when she met Levon the Wolf.

"Stop, fox!" said the wolf. "Give me that duck!"

"No, I won't!"

"I'll take it away from you!"

"If you do, I will tell Governor Kotofei Ivanovich, and he will have you put to death."

"Just who, pray say, is Governor Kotofei Ivanovich?"

"Haven't you heard? He was sent from the Siberian forests to serve as governor of our province. I used to be an old maid, but now I am a governor's wife."

"No, I hadn't heard about that, Elizaveta. May I have a look at him?" asked Levon the Wolf.

"My Kotofei is very cross and cranky. He eats anybody he doesn't like right on the spot. If you wish to see him, you must prepare a sheep and bring it to him as a gift. Put the sheep in a place where it can be seen easily. Then hide so that the governor doesn't see you, for if he does, Brother Levon, you'll have a bad time of it."

The wolf ran off to catch a sheep, and Elizaveta started home again. On the way, she met Mikhailo the Bear. "Stop, fox! Where are you taking that duck? Give it to me!" demanded the bear.

"Step aside, Mikhailo, while you are still in one piece, or else I'll tell Governor Kotofei Ivanovich. He'll have you put to death."

"Just who is Governor Kotofei Ivanovich?" growled the bear.

"He has been sent from the Siberian forests to be our governor. Before he came, I was an old maid. But now I am the wife of our governor."

"May I have a look at him, Elizaveta?" the bear asked the fox.

"My Kotofei is very cross and cranky. He eats anybody who looks at him the wrong way. If you wish to see him, you must prepare an ox and bring it to him as a gift. See that you put the ox in a place where it can be found easily. Then, hide so that the governor doesn't see you, or else you'll have a bad time of it."

Mikhailo the Bear ran off to hunt for an ox, and Elizaveta went home.

By this time, Levon the Wolf had found a sheep and skinned it. He was standing there, lost in thought, when Mikhailo came by, dragging the ox behind him.

"Hello, Mikhailo!" the wolf greeted the bear.

"Hello, Brother Levon. Have you seen Elizaveta's new husband?" asked the bear.

"No, I haven't, Mikhailo, but I am waiting impatiently to meet him."

"Go, call him," the bear said to the wolf.

"No, I won't, Mikhailo. I'm too awkward. You had better call him yourself."

"Nothing doing, Brother Levon. I am rough and clumsy at whatever I do."

Suddenly, as if he had appeared out of nowhere, a rabbit hopped by.

The wolf and bear shouted at him, "Come here, Squint Eyes!" The frightened rabbit, his ears pressed close to his head, crouched down and slunk forward.

"You are nimble and quick on your feet, rabbit. Run over to the fox and tell her that Mikhailo the Bear and Levon the Wolf have been ready for quite some time now and are awaiting her and her new husband, whom they wish to honor with a sheep and an ox."

The rabbit hurried to Elizaveta the Fox as fast as his legs would carry him. Meanwhile, the bear and the wolf looked around for a place to hide.

"I'll climb up this pine tree," said Mikhailo the Bear.

"What will I do? I can't scramble up a tree. Hide me," Levon the Wolf begged the bear.

Mikhailo hid the wolf in some bushes and heaped dry leaves on top of him. Then, the bear climbed up to the very tiptop of a pine tree and watched for Kotofei Ivanovich and Elizaveta the Fox.

The rabbit ran up to the fox's den and said, "Mikhailo the Bear and Levon the Wolf have sent me to say that they have been waiting for quite some time now to honor you and your husband with an ox and a sheep."

"Go away, Squint Eyes. We'll be there in a minute," a gruff voice answered from inside the den. Then, out came the cat and the fox.

When the bear saw them, he said to the wolf, "How tiny our governor is!"

His hair all ruffled, Kotofei Ivanovich rushed over to the ox. He began tearing the meat apart with his teeth and claws, snarling "meow, meow" all the while as if he were angry.

The bear spoke to the wolf again. "He's just tiny, but he eats like a pig. We couldn't eat a fourth of that. Yet, it's little enough as far as he's concerned. Maybe he'll decide to eat us afterward if it isn't enough for him."

Levon the Wolf wanted to see what Governor Kotofei Ivanovich looked like, but he couldn't see through the bushes. He began pushing the leaves aside ever so quietly.

The cat heard the leaves rustling and thought a mouse was moving about. He jumped right at the wolf and grabbed Levon's snout with his claws.

The wolf was frightened. He leaped up and ran for his life.

Catching sight of a fierce wolf instead of the mouse he had expected, Kotofei Ivanovich became frightened, too, and climbed up the very tree in which the bear was sitting.

"Oh, oh," thought Mikhailo, "now he sees me!" The bear looked around, but there was no place to climb. So Mikhailo slid down the tree to the ground, scraping his belly all the way. Then, he jumped up and took to his heels.

Elizaveta the Fox shouted after him, "Run, run, or Kotofei will give you a thrashing!"

The cat and fox lived an easy life that winter with their large store of meat. In fact, they are living an easy life to this very day. Mikhailo the Bear and Levon the Wolf spread the news of the new governor's bad temper throughout the entire forest. Since that time, all of the animals have been afraid of the dreadful Kotofei Ivanovich. They go out of their way to leave him and his wife Elizaveta in peace.

THE WINGED, HAIRY, AND BUTTERY FRIENDS

At the edge of the forest in a warm little cottage, there once lived three friends—a winged sparrow, a hairy mouse, and a buttery pancake called a *blin*. The three had met and become friends after the sparrow flew in from the field, the mouse escaped the cat, and the *blin* ran away from the frying pan.

The sparrow, the mouse, and the *blin* lived together in friendship, never hurting one another's feelings. Each one did his work and helped the others. The sparrow brought his friends food. He brought grain from the fields, mushrooms from the forest, and beans from the garden. The mouse chopped wood, and the *blin* cooked cabbage soup and a porridge called kasha.

So, the three friends lived in harmony. Their routine was like this. After the sparrow returned home from hunting for food, he would wash up with well water and sit on the bench to rest. The mouse would drag in the wood, set the table, and count the painted spoons. Ruddy and fluffy, the *blin* would stand beside the stove salting the cabbage soup and testing the kasha.

When the friends sat down to eat, they could not praise the *blin* enough. The sparrow would say, "Oh, what wonderful cabbage soup. It's fit for nobility, so tasty and rich it is."

The *blin* would reply. "I am a buttery pancake. I plunged into the pot and climbed out again. That is why the cabbage soup is rich."

The sparrow would eat the kasha, praising it, too. "Oh, what splendid kasha this is. It is piping hot."

The mouse would say, "I brought in the wood. I gnawed it into tiny pieces, threw it into the stove, and scattered it around with my tail. That caused it to burn well in the stove. That's why the kasha is hot."

"I was Johnny-on-the-spot, too," the sparrow would say. "I gathered the mushrooms and brought in the beans. That's why you're not hungry."

Thus they lived, praising themselves and one another, and taking no offense.

One day the sparrow became thoughtful. "I fly around the forest all day long," he thought. "I beat my legs and wear out my wings. And what are my friends doing? The *blin* lolls on the stove all morning luxuriating, and sets about making dinner only toward

---

evening. In the morning the mouse carries in wood and gnaws it. Then, she hops up on the stove and turns over on her side and sleeps until dinnertime. But I hunt for food from morning till night. It's hard work. There is no harder work."

The more the sparrow thought, the angrier he got. He stamped his feet, flapped his wings, and began crying, "Tomorrow we'll exchange jobs."

That is just what they did. The *blin* and the mouse understood that it could not be helped, so they decided to swap places. The next morning the *blin* went hunting for food. The sparrow went to chop wood, and the mouse was to cook dinner.

The *blin* rolled off to the forest. It rolled down the road singing:

Hip-hop, hip-hop,
I am buttery sides,
And I can't stop.
I'm mixed with sour cream
And fried in butter.
Hip-hop, hip-hop,
I am a butterball,
And I can't stop.

He ran on and met up with Patrikeevna the Fox.

"Where are you rushing, little *blin*?"

"I'm going hunting."

"What was that song you were singing, little *blin*?"

The pancake hopped in place and began singing:

Hip-hop, hip-hop,
I am buttery sides,
And I can't stop.
I'm mixed with sour cream
And fried in butter.
Hip-hop, hip-hop,
I am a butterball,
And I can't stop.

"You sing very well," said Patrikeevna the Fox as she drew closer to the *blin*. "You say you were mixed with sour cream?"

"With sour cream and sugar," the *blin* answered.

"Hip-hop, you say?" asked the fox. Then she leapt and gave a snort. She snapped her teeth down on the pancake's buttery side.

"Let me go so that I can go to the deep woods to fetch mushrooms and beans," cried the *blin*. "Let me go hunting for food."

"No, I won't let you go," said the fox. "I'll eat you up, gobble you down, sour cream, butter, sugar, and all."

The *blin* struggled and struggled, and scarcely managed to break away from the fox. A piece of its side remained in the fox's teeth, but the rest of the *blin* ran home.

Meanwhile, at home the mouse was cooking cabbage soup. Whatever she put into the soup, whatever she added, made no difference. The soup was not rich, nor tasty, nor buttery.

"How did the *blin* cook cabbage soup?" wondered the mouse. "Oh, yes, now I remember. It dove into the pot and swam around. Then the soup became rich."

The mouse flung herself into the pot. She was scalded terribly. She barely hopped out alive. Her fur coat fell off, and her little tail trembled. She sat on the wooden bench and wept streams of tears.

The sparrow went after wood. He fetched the wood and dragged it home. Then, he began pecking at it in an attempt to break it into tiny pieces. He pecked and pecked until his beak turned to the side. He sat on the *zavalinka*, which is a mound of earth piled around a Russian peasant cottage to protect against severe weather, and wept streams of tears.

The *blin* came running home and saw the sparrow sitting on the *zavalinka* with his beak twisted to one side and weeping.

The *blin* ran into the cottage and saw the mouse sitting on the bench without her fur coat and with her tail trembling. When the mouse saw that the *blin*'s side was eaten away, she wept all the louder.

"This is what happens when one lays blame on another and doesn't want to do his own work," said the *blin*.

In shame, the sparrow took refuge beneath the wooden bench.

Nothing was to be done. The friends wept and grieved. Then, they began living again in the old manner. The sparrow fetched the food. The mouse chopped the wood. The *blin* prepared the cabbage soup and kasha.

Thus they live to this day, gnawing on honey cakes, drinking mead, and remembering you and me.

THE LION, THE PIKE, AND MAN

Once upon a time a pike and a lion were conversing. The lion stood on the riverbank while talking to the pike, who was frolicking in the river. A man came along and stood a distance away listening to their conversation.

When the pike saw the man, she immediately went off deeper into the river.

The next day when the lion saw the pike again, he asked, "Why did you go away yesterday?"

"I saw Man."

"Well, what of it?"

"Oh, Man is a cunning creature."

"Man is nothing," said the lion. "Give him to me and I'll eat him up. I'm going to look for him to do just that."

Then, the lion set out in search of Man. He met a little boy. "Are you Man?" he asked the child.

"No, I'm not a man yet. I'm a little boy. Someday I'll be a man."

When the lion learned that the boy was not Man, he did not touch him, but traveled on. He came upon an old man. "Are you Man?" the lion asked.

"No, Father Lion. What kind of man would I make? I was a man once, though."

The lion did not touch the old man. "How puzzling," he said. "I can't find Man anywhere."

The lion walked on and met a soldier carrying a rifle and a saber. "Are you Man?" asked the lion.

"I'm Man," the soldier replied.

"Well, I'm going to eat you up!"

"Very well, but wait just a moment," said the soldier. "Move back away from me, and I'll leap right into your jaws. Open your mouth as wide as you can."

The lion moved back, opening his mouth wide. The soldier took aim with his rifle, and there was a bang. Then, he ran up to the lion with his saber and cut off the lion's ear. The lion took to his heels.

He ran to the river. The pike came swimming and asked, "Well, did you see Man?"

"You were right," said the lion, "Man is cunning. I couldn't find him right away. One creature said that he had been Man, and another said he would become Man. When I finally met Man, it was no joy. He ordered me to stand back and open my jaws. Then, he spit into my mouth, and my mouth is still stinging. Next, Man stuck out his tongue and licked off my ear."

"Didn't I tell you that Man is cunning?" asked the pike.

CHEEKY THE GOAT

There once lived a woman and a man. The woman had a daughter, and the man had a daughter.

One day the man bought a goat and ordered the woman's daughter to take the goat to pasture.

The woman's daughter stayed all day in the pasture with the goat. Toward evening, she gave the goat some water and drove her home.

The man was waiting for the girl at the gate. "Did you get enough to eat and drink, my dear little goat?" he asked.

The goat answered like this:

No, sir, I neither ate, nor drank.
While running across a little bridge,
I grabbed a maple leaf. Just think,
While running across a little dyke,
I sipped a drop of water; it was rank.
That's all I ate, all I drank.

The man was angry with the woman's daughter and he scolded her severely.

The next day he sent his own daughter. "Take the goat to the field, daughter, and see that she is well fed and watered."

The man's daughter stayed in the pasture with the goat all day long. Toward evening she gave the goat some water to drink and drove it home.

The man was waiting by the gate. "Did you get enough to eat and drink, my dear little goat?" he asked.

Once again the goat said:

No, sir, I neither ate, nor drank.
While running across a little bridge,
I grabbed a maple leaf. Just think,
While running across a little dyke,

I sipped a drop of water; it was rank.

That's all I ate, all I drank.

The man got angry and he scolded his daughter.

The third day, the man decided to go himself. He drove the goat into the field. The goat stayed in the pasture all day long. In the evening, the man gave the goat some water and drove her home.

The man ran home ahead of the goat and stood by the gate waiting for her. When the goat returned, the man asked, "Goat, my dear little goat, did you get enough to eat and drink?"

Once again the goat sang her little song.

No, sir, I neither ate, nor drank.

While running across a little bridge,

I grabbed a maple leaf. Just think,

While running across a little dyke,

I sipped a drop of water; it was rank.

That's all I ate, all I drank.

"Liar! So that's what you're like!" exclaimed the man. He grabbed the goat by the horns and disciplined her.

The goat broke away from the man and ran into the forest. She ran on without looking back. She came upon a rabbit's cottage in the forest. The goat ran inside. The rabbit was not at home, so the goat locked the door and got up on to the stove, where it was warm and where only the sick and elderly are allowed to lie.

A little later the rabbit came home. He grabbed the door handle with his paw, but the door was locked. "Who's there?" asked the rabbit.

The goat sang from the stove:

I'm Cheeky the Goat.

I cost three half-copecks.*

On one side I'm fleeced.

I'll stamp with my feet,

Butt with my horns,

Kick with my feet,

Flail with my tail,

Until you are gone.

When he heard what the goat said, the rabbit was afraid. Some strange beast was staying in his little cottage. The rabbit sat under a birch tree and wept.

A gray wolf who was passing by asked, "Why are you crying, Rabbit?"

---

*Copecks were to the ruble what a penny is to the dollar.

"How could I not cry? Cheeky the Goat has settled into my home, and she has locked the door. Now I have nowhere to live."

"Don't cry, Rabbit," said the wolf. "I'll drive away that beast for you."

The wolf went up to the rabbit's little cottage and asked, "Who is staying in Rabbit's cottage?"

The goat sang out from her comfortable, warm spot atop the stove.

I'm Cheeky the Goat.

I cost three half-copecks.

On one side I'm fleeced.

I'll stamp with my feet,

Butt with my horns,

Kick with my feet,

Flail with my tail,

Until you are gone.

When he heard the goat's threats, the wolf took to his heels. Once again the rabbit sat down beneath the birch tree and wept.

Then, a bear came by. "Why are you crying, Rabbit?" he asked.

"Why wouldn't I cry? Cheeky the Goat has settled in my cottage and locked the door. I have nowhere to live now."

"Don't cry, Rabbit," said the bear. "I'll drive away that beast."

The bear went up to the little hut and roared, "Who is staying in Rabbit's cottage?"

The goat sang out from her perch atop the stove.

I am Cheeky the Goat.

I cost three half-copecks.

On one side I'm fleeced.

I'll stamp with my feet,

Butt with my horns,

Kick with my feet,

Flail with my tail,

Until you are gone.

The bear took fright. He had never heard of such a beast. He had never seen such a beast. He ran away into the forest.

Once again, the rabbit sat down beneath the birch tree and wept bitterly.

A bee came flying. "Why are you crying, Rabbit?"

The rabbit told the bee about his misfortune.

"Don't grieve, Rabbit. I'll help you," said the bee.

"How can you help me, bee? The wolf tried to drive away the goat, and couldn't. The bear tried to drive her away, and couldn't. How can you get rid of the goat?"

The bee did not answer. Instead, she flew up to the rabbit's little cottage and asked, "Who is living in this little cottage?"

The goat sang out from atop the stove.

I am Cheeky the Goat.
I cost three half-copecks.
On one side I'm fleeced.
I'll stamp with my feet,
Butt with my horns,
Kick with my feet,
Flail with my tail,
Until you are gone.

The bee was not afraid. She began flying around the cottage, peeking into all the chinks. She buzzed and buzzed until she found a little hole. She crawled through the hole and entered the cottage. Then, she flew up to the goat and stung her on the side that had been fleeced.

The goat rushed to the door and ran off into the forest, so fast that she could not be seen for greased lightning.

The rabbit rejoiced. He ran into his cottage and lived there happily ever after.

PART 2

FAIRY TALES

THE SNOW MAIDEN

There once lived an old woman and an old man. They lived in harmony and friendship. Everything would have been fine, had it not been for a great sorrow—the old couple had no children.

One winter, so much snow fell that the snowdrifts formed up to one's waist. Village children spilled out onto the street to play. Through the window, the old woman and the old man watched them playing, and they sadly thought about their longing for a child.

"What about it, old woman, let's make a daughter out of snow," the old man proposed.

"Let's," the old woman replied.

The old man put on his hat. The couple went into the garden and began fashioning a daughter out of snow. They rolled a large snowball and placed little arms and little legs on it. Then, they stuck a head made of snow on top. The old man fashioned a nose, a rosebud mouth, and a chin.

As they looked at their creation, the Snow Maiden's lips grew rosy and her eyes opened. She looked at the old couple and smiled. Then, she began nodding her head and moving her arms and legs. She shook off the snow, and a living girl walked out of the snowdrift.

The old couple rejoiced. They took the Snow Maiden into their cottage. They kept looking at her, and their eyes and hearts could not get their fill of looking.

The little girl grew not by days, but by hours. With the passing of each day, she became more beautiful. Her light-brown braid hung to her waist. She had no color at all, for she was white as snow.

The old people doted on their daughter. They had not expected that she would have a soul, since she was made of snow, after all. But their daughter grew to be wise and thoughtful and merry. She was kind and friendly to everyone. Whatever the Snow Maiden undertook went well. When she sang a song, everyone stopped to listen, so beautifully did she sing.

Winter passed, and the spring sun began warming the earth. Green grass appeared on the patches of earth where the snow had melted. The larks began singing. Suddenly, the Snow Maiden grew sad.

"What is wrong, Daughter?" asked the old couple. "Why have you become so melancholy? Aren't you feeling well?"

The Snow Maiden

"It's nothing, Father. It's nothing, Mother. I am well," the girl said.

Finally, the last of the snow melted. The flowers were blooming in the meadows, and the birds were flying overhead.

With each passing day, the Snow Maiden became sadder and more silent. She hid from the sun. She preferred the cool shade, and she was particularly happy when it rained.

One day a black cloud approached and spilled large balls of hail onto the earth. The Snow Maiden rejoiced over the hail, which looked like pearls raining down.

When the sun peeked out again and the hail melted, the Snow Maiden burst into tears. She wept bitterly, as a sister weeps over the loss of a brother.

After the passing of spring, summer came. The girls of the village got ready to walk to the forest. They called to the Snow Maiden. "Come with us, Snow Maiden, to stroll in the forest and to sing songs and dance."

"Go ahead, Daughter. Have a good time with your friends," said the old woman.

The Snow Maiden and her friends went to the forest. They picked flowers and wove wreaths. They sang songs and danced the *khorovod*, which is a round dance. Only the Snow Maiden was melancholy.

When it grew dark, they gathered some twigs and made a bonfire. They began jumping, one after another, over the fire. The Snow Maiden stood behind the others, last in line.

When it was the Snow Maiden's turn, she began running. She ran quickly and jumped over the fire, and—suddenly she melted, turning into a soft white cloud.

The white cloud drifted and rose high into the sky. As the cloud flew away, the Snow Maiden's friends heard a plaintive moaning behind them, which sounded like "oh!"

The children turned around and began looking in the direction whence the moan had come, but the Snow Maiden was nowhere to be seen.

They called and called. "Halloo, halloo! Answer us, Snow Maiden!"

But only the echo of their voices resounding throughout the forest was heard.

TERYOSHECHKA

There once lived an old woman and an old man who had no children. They had lived for a long, long time, but still no child was born, no matter how hard they wished.

Finally, they carved a little boy out of a log. They put a diaper and swaddling clothes on the wooden figure. Then they began rocking the log as they sang a lullaby.

Sleep, little Teryoshechka, sleep.

The swallows are asleep.

The martens make no peep.

The foxes, too, are sleeping,

And they wish for small Teryoshechka

A good sleep, sound and deep.

They kept rocking the log and singing lullabies to it until one day they looked in the cradle and there was no log at all. The log had become a real little boy, and he was ever so handsome.

The boy grew in stature and reason. One day the old man made a canoe for his little son. He painted the canoe white and the oars red.

The old man took the canoe to the lake. Little Teryoshechka sat in the canoe and commanded, "Canoe, sail on!"

The canoe sailed far from shore to the middle of the lake. Little Teryoshechka began fishing in the lake.

His mother brought him milk and cottage cheese for lunch. She stood on the shore and called, "Teryoshechka, my son, sail ashore. I've brought you something to eat and drink."

Teryoshechka heard his mother's voice from afar. He sailed ashore. His mother took the fish he had caught and gave him the cottage cheese and milk. She changed his shirt and let him go back to his fishing.

Baba Yaga, the Russian witch, found out about Teryoshechka. She came to the shore of the lake and called in a terrifying voice, "Teryoshechka, my son, sail ashore. I've brought you something to eat and drink."

Teryoshechka knew right away that it was not his mother's voice. "Canoe, sail far away. That is not Mother calling me," he said.

Baba Yaga decided to trick Teryoshechka. She ran to the blacksmith and ordered him to forge her a new throat so that her voice would become like the voice of Teryoshechka's mother, gentle and sweet.

The blacksmith forged the witch a new throat. Baba Yaga rushed to the shore of the lake and began singing in a voice exactly like that of Teryoshechka's mother. "Teryoshechka, my son, sail ashore. I've brought you something to eat and drink."

Teryoshechka recognized his mother's voice and sailed ashore. Baba Yaga grabbed the boy. She put him in a sack and set off running.

She brought him to her cottage on chicken legs. There, she ordered her daughter, Alyonka, to heat the oven hot and to roast Teryoshechka for dinner.

Baba Yaga left them and rushed off to find more victims.

Alyonka heated the oven ever so hot. "Lie down on the wooden oven shovel that I use for loading and unloading loaves of bread, so that I can put you into the oven," she ordered.

Teryoshechka sat on the shovel. He spread out his arms and legs so that he could not fit into the oven.

"Don't lie like that," said Alyonka.

"But I don't know how to lie. Show me," said Teryoshechka.

"Lie there like cats and dogs lie when they are sleeping," said Alyonka.

"You lie down and show me," said the boy.

Alyonka sat on the shovel, and Teryoshechka pushed the shovel into the oven and shut the oven door. Then, he went out of the cottage and climbed into a tall oak tree.

Baba Yaga came home. She opened the oven and pulled out Alyonka. However, she did not know it was her daughter, so she ate her up and swallowed even the bones.

Then, she went into the yard and began rolling in the grass. As she rolled, she said, "I'm rolling in the grass after having eaten Teryoshechka's meat."

"Roll all you want, but it is Alyonka's meat that you have eaten," Teryoshechka said from his perch in the oak tree.

"Could that be the leaves rustling?" asked Baba Yaga.

Then, she took up her former chant. "I'm rolling in the grass after eating Teryoshechka's meat."

Teryoshechka, too, intoned, "Roll all you want, but you have eaten the meat of your own daughter, Alyonka."

The witch glanced up and saw Teryoshechka high up in the oak tree. Enraged, she set about gnawing the tree. She gnawed until she broke her two upper front teeth.

She ran to the blacksmith. "Blacksmith," she cried, "forge me two iron teeth."

The blacksmith did as she ordered, and Baba Yaga returned to gnaw on the oak tree again. She gnawed until she broke her two lower front teeth.

Again, she rushed off to the blacksmith. "Blacksmith, forge me another two iron teeth."

The blacksmith made two lower teeth for her. Baba Yaga returned to the oak tree and started gnawing. As she gnawed, chips of wood flew. The oak began shaking and swaying.

What could little Teryoshechka do? He saw some swan-geese flying overhead. "Swan-geese, please take me on your wings and carry me to Mother and Father," he begged.

"Honk, honk," answered the swan-geese. "Other geese are following us. They will take you."

The witch gnawed on. She stopped to glance at Teryoshechka and smacked her lips. Then, she set about gnawing again.

Another flock of swan-geese came flying. "Swan-geese, please take me on your wings and carry me to Mother and Father," Teryoshechka begged.

"Honk, honk," answered the swan-geese. "Pincers the Swan-Goose is following us. He'll take you."

The witch had only a little bit more to gnaw. The oak was already beginning to fall.

Pincers the Swan-Goose came flying.

"Swan-goose, please take me on your wings and carry me to Mother and Father," Teryoshechka begged.

Pincers the Swan-Goose took pity on Teryoshechka. He seated the boy on his back. Then he beat his wings and flew off, carrying Teryoshechka home.

Pincers flew to Teryoshechka's cottage and landed on the grass.

The old woman was cooking pancakes in preparation for a memorial service in memory of Teryoshechka, whom the old couple thought was dead. "Here's a pancake for you, old man, and this one's for me."

"And where's my pancake?" asked Teryoshechka, who was sitting beneath the window.

The old woman heard his voice. "Old man, go find out who is asking for a pancake," she said.

The old man went out and saw Teryoshechka sitting there. He brought the boy to the old woman. When the old woman saw her son, there were many kisses and hugs and much happiness and rejoicing.

Pincers the Swan-Goose was given food and drink, and then set free. From that day on, Pincers flapped his wings proudly. He flew at the beginning, rather than the end, of the formation. Remembering his adventure with Teryoshechka, he grew strong and brave and became the leader of the flock.

FATHER FROST

There once lived a man who had married for the second time. His second wife had a daughter of her own, and he had a daughter of his own.

Everyone knows what it is like to live with some stepmothers. Whichever way one turns, whatever one does, one is scolded and disciplined. Whatever the stepmother's own daughter does, she is patted on the head and called "clever girl."

The little stepdaughter fed and watered the cattle. She carried wood and water into the cottage. She started the fire in the stove and swept the cottage. And she did everything before dawn.

Yet, she could not please her stepmother. Nothing was as her stepmother wanted—everything was wrong. Even if the wind began making a noise while blowing and then immediately grew silent, the mean stepmother would become disagreeable and ask when the wind was going to calm down.

One day the woman decided to cause her stepdaughter's death. "Take her! Take her away, old man," she said to her husband. "Take her wherever you wish, just so that I never lay eyes on her again. Take her to the forest, to the bitter frost, to freeze to death."

The old man began grieving. He burst into tears, but nothing could be done. He could not outargue the woman. So, he harnessed the horse to the sleigh. "Get into the sleigh, dear daughter," he said.

The old man took his daughter to the forest. He put her down in a snowdrift under a big fir tree and left her there.

Shivering, the girl sat beneath the fir tree. A cruel chill penetrated her clothing. Suddenly, she heard Father Frost crackling through the fir trees, leaping and snapping among the branches, not far away.

He came up to the fir under which the girl was sitting and from the top of the tree he asked, "Are you warm, little maiden?"

The little girl did not want to complain to Father Frost. She thought that it would be impolite. "I'm warm, Father Frost, I'm warm," she answered.

Father Frost descended and came closer, crackling and snapping all the more. "*Now* are you warm, little maiden? Are you warm, my little beauty, or are you turning red from the cold?"

The girl could scarcely take a breath. "It's warm, Father Frost, it's warm," she said.

Father Frost descended and drew even closer. He began crackling and snapping even more. "*Now* are you warm, girl? Are you warm, my little beauty? Are you warm, my little darling?"

The little maiden had begun to turn to stone. She could barely move her tongue, but she did not lose patience with Father Frost. "Oh, I'm warm, dear Father Frost."

Then, and only then, did Father Frost take pity on the little maiden. He wrapped her in warm fur coats and warmed her with down-filled quilts.

Meanwhile, the stepmother, thinking that her stepdaughter was dead, was cooking pancakes (*bliny*) for the girl's wake. "Go get your daughter, you old fogey, and bring her back to be buried," she said to the old man.

Sadly, the old man went to the forest. He came to the spot where he had left his daughter. Merry and rosy-cheeked, she was sitting beneath the big fir tree adorned in silver and gold jewelry and wearing a sable coat. A chest filled with luxurious gifts stood nearby.

The old man rejoiced. He placed his daughter's gifts in the sleigh. Then, he lifted the girl into the sleigh and took her home.

At home the old woman was making pancakes as the little dog lay under the table. "Bow-wow, the old man's daughter is coming all adorned in silver and gold," said the little dog. "She will make a beautiful bride, but no one wants to marry the old woman's daughter."

The old woman threw a pancake (*blin*) to the dog. "Don't bark such nonsense. Say that the old woman's daughter will marry, but that only the bones of the old man's daughter will be brought home."

The dog ate the pancake. Once again, the dog began barking. "Bow-wow! The old man's daughter is coming adorned in silver and gold. She will make a beautiful bride, but no one wants to marry the old woman's daughter."

The old woman threw some more pancakes to the dog and scolded her, but the dog kept repeating one and the same thing.

Suddenly, the gate creaked. The door opened and the stepdaughter entered the cottage. She was radiant and adorned in silver and gold. The old man followed, carrying a deep and heavy chest.

The old woman looked at the little maiden and threw up her hands. She saw how beautiful her stepdaughter was and how many gifts she had brought home, and she was envious. She wanted the same for her own daughter. "Old fogey, harness the other horse," she ordered. "Take my daughter to the forest and put her down at the same spot."

The old man lifted the old woman's daughter into the sleigh. He took her to the forest, to the very same spot. He placed her in a snowdrift beneath the tall fir tree and left.

The old woman's daughter sat there, her teeth chattering. Father Frost came crackling through the forest, leaping from tree to tree and snapping the branches.

He looked at the old woman's daughter. "Are you warm, little maiden?" he asked.

"Oh, it's freezing!" she replied. "Don't crackle and crunch so, Father Frost."

Father Frost descended from the treetop and drew nearer. He crackled and snapped all the more. "Are you warm, little maiden?" he asked. "Are you warm, my little beauty?"

"Oh, my hands and feet are frozen. Go away, Father Frost," whined the stepsister.

Father Frost descended and came even nearer. He crackled, snapped, and struck all the harder.

"*Now* are you warm, little maiden? Are you warm, my little beauty?"

"Oh, I'm freezing cold! Don't crackle and crunch, Father Frost."

Father Frost descended even lower. He crackled and snapped even more. "*Now* are you warm, little maiden? Are you warm, my little beauty?"

The stepsister lost all patience with Father Frost. "Oh, I'm completely frozen," she complained. "Get out of my sight! Get lost! Curse you, Father Frost!"

Father Frost became angry. He grabbed the old woman's daughter and held her until she froze to death.

At the crack of dawn, the old woman said to her husband, "Harness the horse quickly, old fogey, and go fetch my daughter. Bring her to me adorned in silver and gold."

The old man set out. The little dog lying under the table barked, "Bow-wow! The old man's daughter will marry, but the bones of the old woman's daughter will be brought home in a sack."

The old woman threw a pie to the dog. "Don't bark such nonsense. Say, 'The old woman's daughter will be brought home adorned in silver and gold.' "

But the dog kept barking, "Bow-wow! The bones of the old woman's daughter will be brought home in a sack."

The gate creaked, and the old woman rushed to greet her daughter. She turned over the matting on the floor of the sleigh. Her daughter was lying there dead. The old woman began wailing and crying, but it was too late—she had lost her daughter.

Children in the town of Orel, in the heart of Russia, pose for the photographer.

A grandmother displays her handiwork.

Spinning yarn on a distaff (*prialka*), a staff on which fibers are wound before being spun into thread.

Children in a playhouse constructed to look like the hut on chicken legs of Baba Yaga, the Russian witch. Pine Forest Tourist Center (*Sosnovyi bor*) near Kostroma.

Playmates Vaska the Cat and hen friend outside a country home.

A six-year-old girl chants *chastushki,* four-line rhymed verses.

A dancer at the "Festival Landmarks" (*Vekhi*) in the Kostroma Museum of Folk Architecture and Folk Life (1993).

Young folk dancers performing in the village of Nerekhta, near Kostroma.

The Russian stove can occupy as much as a fifth of a room.

A decorative Russian samovar. A teapot containing a concentrated tea brew (*zavarka*) is placed on top of the samovar. A small amount of the brew is poured into a glass with a holder (*podstakannik*). Finally, water is poured from the spout to dilute the tea.

A collection of nesting dolls (*matrioshki*). From left to right, the first two dolls are traditional in style. The third doll was made by Udmurts. The fourth and fifth dolls have religious motifs. The doll on the far right depicts Boris Yeltsin, President of Russia from 1992–2000.

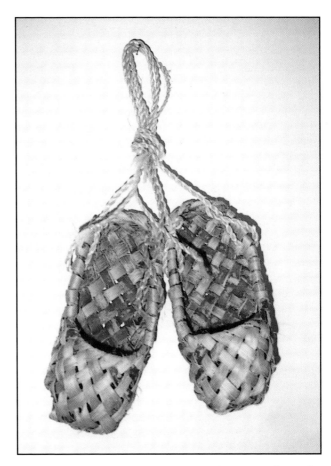

Hand-woven *lapti,* bast shoes or sandals made from the fibers of the linden tree.

Sliding down an icy knoll outside a Moscow apartment building.

Young admirers of Western culture relaxing on the Arbat in Moscow.

A St. Petersburg bazaar.

Eighteenth-century Church of the Savior from the village of Fominskoe. The church is now located in the Kostroma Museum of Folk Architecture and Folk Life.

Modern *dacha* (summer house) outside Moscow.

The older section of the village of Lopatino, unchanged by modern progress.

St. Basil's Cathedral in Moscow is a unique and whimsical cathedral. It was built in 1555–1561 by Ivan the Terrible to commemorate the taking of Kazan.

The Moscow Kremlin. The original meaning of the word *kremlin* (*kreml'*) indicated a fortress surrounding a town.

PIGSKIN

There once lived a prince who had a stepdaughter named Nastasia. The girl and her mother, the princess, were alike as two peas in a pod both in looks and in behavior. When the princess died, the prince decided to marry his stepdaughter.

"Nastasia, dear," he said, "I'm going to marry you!"

Nastasia did not want to marry her stepfather, the prince, so as a condition to their marriage she thought up a difficult task for him. "If you wish to marry me," she said, "you must buy me a dress sprinkled with stars and constellations. If you don't find a dress like that, I won't marry you."

The prince found a dress resplendent with stars and constellations, just as Nastasia had described, and he bought it for her. When Nastasia put on the dress, she was so beautiful that the prince wanted to marry her all the more.

"Let's get married, Nastasia," he said.

The girl thought for a while. Then, she said, "Buy me a dress with the moon on the back and a beautiful sun on the front. Only then will I marry you."

The prince bought Nastasia the dress she had described and once again asked her to marry him.

Nastasia was still unwilling to marry her stepfather. She considered how she might escape the distasteful union. Finally she said, "Order that a pigskin be made for me."

The prince ordered that the pigskin be made. As soon as the prince's servants brought Nastasia the pigskin, she put it on. When the prince saw how ugly Nastasia looked in the pigskin, he spit on her and drove her from his palace. He did not give her even a crust of bread for the road.

Nastasia went out the gate and set out in whichever direction her nose led. She walked for one day, two days, three days—until she came to a foreign land.

Suddenly, storm clouds drew near and a thunderstorm arose. Where could Nastasia hide from the rain?

Nastasia noticed a tall oak tree. She climbed up and sat among its thick branches.

Meanwhile, Prince Ivan was in the forest hunting. As he was passing the oak tree, his dogs rushed to the tree and began barking. Prince Ivan was curious to learn why his dogs were barking at the oak tree. He sent his servant to have a look.

The servant returned and said, "A beast is sitting in the oak tree. It's not really a beast, but some sort of miraculous creature."

Prince Ivan approached the tree. "What kind of wonder are you? Do you speak?" he asked.

"I am Pigskin," answered Nastasia.

The prince called a halt to the hunt and seated Pigskin in his carriage. "I'll take her home to Mother and Father," he thought.

When they saw Pigskin, the king and queen "oohed" and "aahed" and marveled at the extraordinary wonder. Then, they sent Pigskin off to the kitchen to sit behind the stove.

After some time had passed, the king began preparing for a ball. All of the courtiers were invited to the ball to make merry and to enjoy themselves.

"May I stand by the door and watch the dancing?" Pigskin asked the king's servant.

"Why on earth would you want to do that, Pigskin?" replied the servant.

Nastasia paid no heed to the servant's words. She walked to the open field and arrayed herself in her shining dress that was decorated with stars and constellations. She gave a whistle and a shout, and a carriage appeared from nowhere. She got into the carriage and set out for the ball.

Immediately upon arrival, she began dancing. Everyone was amazed and wondered where such a beauty had come from. Nastasia danced the evening away.

After dancing to her heart's content, she changed into her pigskin and hid. She returned to her spot behind the stove.

The next morning Prince Ivan came to her and asked jokingly, "Wasn't it you last night, Pigskin? Weren't you the beautiful maiden who danced all evening?"

"It wouldn't do for me to dance in my pigskin. I just stood by the door," she answered.

At the king's palace, they prepared for a second evening of dancing and merrymaking.

Once again Pigskin asked the king's servant if she might watch the festivities. Once again the servant answered, "Why on earth would you want to do that, Pigskin?"

Nastasia went to the open field, as she had done before. She gave a whistle and a shout, and a carriage appeared. Nastasia shed her ugly pigskin and put on the dress with the moon glowing on the back and the sun shining on the front.

She went to the ball and began dancing. Once again, she hid after she had danced her fill.

Prince Ivan noticed the absence of the transformed Pigskin. "What shall we do?" he asked. "How can I find out who that beautiful maiden is?"

He came up with an idea. He ordered that the first step of the palace staircase be tarred so that the unknown maiden's slipper would stick to it.

When Nastasia arrived at the ball on the third evening, she seemed even more beautiful to everyone there. She danced the evening away, but when she started to leave the palace, her slipper stuck to the tar.

Prince Ivan took the slipper and began searching for the person it fit. He traveled around his entire kingdom, but the slipper fit no one.

Then, he had an idea. He went home to the palace and searched for Pigskin. When he found her, he ordered, "Show me your feet."

Nastasia showed him her feet. Prince Ivan measured the slipper to her foot—and saw that it was just right. He grabbed a knife and slit the pigskin, which he threw away.

Then, he took Nastasia's white hand and led her to his mother and father, whose permission he asked to marry Nastasia. His parents gave the couple their blessing.

Nastasia and Prince Ivan were married. After they married, Prince Ivan asked, "Why did you wear a pigskin?"

"My stepfather wanted to marry me. But when I put on the pigskin, he no longer desired me. I kept wearing it because it kept him away from me," Nastasia explained.

From then on Nastasia and Prince Ivan lived in happiness. The evil stepfather never bothered them again.

THE SILVER SAUCER AND THE RED APPLE

There once lived a peasant and his wife. They had three daughters, and all three were beautiful. However, the two older girls were lazy and vain. They spent all their time primping and preening. The third and youngest daughter, Alyonushka, was a good girl and a hard worker. She was the most beautiful of them all.

Alyonushka took care of everything. She tidied the cottage and prepared the meals. She weeded the garden and fetched the water. She was kind to her parents and friendly to her neighbors. Her mother and father loved her dearly. That made her older sisters jealous.

One day the mother and father went to the field to mow hay. While they were gone, a poor old woman came to the cottage begging for bread. The older sisters did not want to talk to her, but Alyonushka gave the old woman a bun and walked a short way past the gate with her.

"Thank you, fair maiden," the old woman said. "I will repay you for your kindness with some good advice. When your father goes to the fair, ask him to buy a silver saucer and a red apple for you to play with. Roll the apple on the saucer and repeat:

Roll, roll, little apple,

Round my silver saucer.

As I watch,

Let there be

Towns and fields,

Woods and seas,

Mountains high,

And rosy skies.

If ever you should be in need, fair maiden, I will help you. Just remember that I live in the deep, dark forest. It takes exactly three days and three nights to reach my cottage." Having spoken these words, the old woman disappeared among the trees.

After some time had passed, the peasant got ready to go to the fair. "What gifts shall I buy you?" he asked his daughters.

"Buy me some red calico so that I can make myself a sarafan,* Father," the eldest said.

"Buy me some cotton with a pretty design," the middle daughter requested.

When Alyonushka's turn came, she said, "My dear father, buy me a silver saucer and a red apple."

The peasant promised to fulfill his daughters' wishes and set out for the fair. When he came back, he gave his daughters their gifts. He had bought cotton with a pretty design for the middle daughter, red calico for his eldest daughter, and a silver saucer and a red apple for Alyonushka. The older sisters rejoiced over their gifts and laughed at Alyonushka, waiting to see what she would do with the silver saucer and red apple.

Alyonushka did not eat the apple. Instead, she sat in a corner and rolled the apple round and round the saucer, while repeating:

Roll, roll, little apple,

Round my silver saucer.

As I watch,

Let there be

Towns and fields,

Woods and seas,

Mountains high,

And rosy skies.

The apple rolled around the saucer, its red skin reflected in the silver dish. When Alyonushka looked into the saucer, she saw tiny villages bordering wide fields, ships on blue seas, towns, high mountains, and rosy skies. The bright sun and the silvery moon whirled round and round. Stars gathered and danced in a ring. Everything was more marvelous than a story could tell or a pen could describe.

Her sisters stared in wonder at the magic saucer, and they were envious. They wanted to persuade Alyonushka to give the saucer and apple to them, but Alyonushka would not swap her treasure for anything.

Then, the sisters schemed to take away the saucer and apple by trickery and force. "Dear, dear Alyonushka, let's go to the forest. We'll pick some strawberries there," they coaxed.

Alyonushka agreed. She gave the saucer and apple to her father for safekeeping and went with her sisters. As she picked berries, Alyonushka wandered through trees and bushes. Her sisters led her farther and farther away from home. They took her into the deepest part of the forest, and there they fell upon her and killed her. The evil girls buried Alyonushka under a birch tree and returned home to their mother and father late that night.

"Alyonushka ran away from us and got lost," they lied. "We combed the entire forest, but we couldn't find her. The wolves must have eaten her."

---

*A sarafan is similar to a long pinafore or jumper.

The Silver Saucer and the Red Apple   71

Alyonushka's mother and father shed bitter tears. The sisters begged their father for the silver saucer and the red apple. "No," he said sadly. "I won't give the saucer and apple to anyone. They will be a reminder to me of Alyonushka, my beloved daughter." Then he put the magic apple and saucer into a small chest and locked it.

One day at dawn, a long time afterward, a shepherd was driving his flock of sheep past the deep forest. A little lamb lagged behind and ran off among the trees. As the shepherd was walking through the forest in search of his lamb, he came upon a slender, white birch. Under it was a little mound. On top of the mound and all around it were scarlet and azure flowers. A thin reed was growing high above the flowers.

The shepherd cut the reed and made himself a little pipe. Miracle of miracles and wonder of wonders, the pipe began playing a song of its own. It sang:

Play, play, little shepherd,

Play softly,

Play sweetly.

Unhappy am I

So early to die.

They've killed me

And laid me

Beneath the birch tree.

They wanted my saucer

And apple, you see.

As the shepherd approached the village, the pipe kept singing its song. The villagers listened in wonder and began asking the shepherd questions about the meaning of the song.

"Good people," said the shepherd, "I know nothing. I was searching for my lamb in the forest when I noticed a little mound. There were flowers on the mound, and growing high above the flowers was a reed. I cut the reed and made myself a pipe. The pipe plays and speaks by itself."

Alyonushka's mother and father happened to be among the crowd. They listened to the shepherd's story. The mother grabbed the pipe, and it started singing. It said:

Play, play, darling mother,

Play softly,

Play sweetly.

Unhappy am I

So early to die.

They've killed me

And laid me

Beneath the birch tree.

They wanted my saucer

And apple, you see.

The pipe's words broke the hearts of Alyonushka's parents. "Shepherd, take us to the place where you cut the reed," said the father.

The shepherd led Alyonushka's mother and father into the forest, and the villagers followed. They saw the birch and the little mound covered with scarlet and azure flowers. When they dug into the mound, they found the murdered Alyonushka.

The parents recognized their beloved daughter and wept inconsolably. "Good people, who killed her?" they asked.

Alyonushka's father took the pipe, and it started singing. It said:

Play, play, dearest father,

Play softly,

Play sweetly.

Unhappy am I

So early to die.

My sisters

Have laid me

Beneath the birch tree.

They wanted my saucer

And apple, you see.

The pipe told Alyonushka's father to go into the deep forest and keep walking until he came to a wooden cottage where the kind old woman who had befriended Alyonushka earlier lived. According to the pipe's instructions, she would give him a flask filled with the water of life. He had only to sprinkle Alyonushka with the water, and she would wake from her deep sleep of death.

Alyonushka's mother and father set out on their journey through the deep, dark forest. They walked for exactly three days and three nights and finally came to a cottage. An old, old woman came out onto the porch, and Alyonushka's parents asked her for the water of life.

"I will help Alyonushka," said the old woman. "I will help her because she has a kind heart."

The old woman gave the couple a flask filled with the water of life and said, "Pour a handful of your native soil into the flask. Without it, the water has no power."

Bowing down to the ground in front of the old woman, the mother and father thanked her. Then, they returned the way they had come.

When they got to the village, they poured a handful of their native soil into the flask, just as the old woman had ordered. They took the evil sisters with them and went into the forest. The people of the village followed them.

The father sprinkled the water of life on Alyonushka, and she came alive. The evil sisters were frightened. Their faces turned white, and they confessed to everything. Their neighbors grabbed them, tied them up, and took them back to the village.

People gathered around. They decided that the sisters should be given a terrible punishment for what they had done. They sent the evil girls away from their home and ordered them never to return. Alyonushka began living with her mother and father as before, and they loved her more than ever.

THE PUFF MONSTER

There once lived a woman and a man who had two children. The girl's name was Manya, and the boy's name was Vanya.

One day the couple got ready to go to town. Before leaving, they gave the following instructions. "Don't go to the cellar, children. If you do, the Puff Monster will eat you up."

After their parents had left, Vanya said, "Manya, I'm going to the cellar. Dad keeps lots of turnips down there. I love turnips. We'll get some and cook them for lunch."

No sooner had Vanya gone down into the cellar than the Puff Monster emerged from a dark corner. "I am the Puff Monster. Are you Vanya who has come to get some turnips? Shall I eat you up? Shall I gobble you down?

"Gobble, gobble!" said the Puff Monster, and he ate up Vanya. After eating the boy, the Puff Monster grew to twice his normal size.

When Vanya failed to return, Manya went to the cellar to get him.

The Puff Monster came out of his dark corner. "I am the Puff Monster," he said. "Are you Manya who has come for Vanya, who came to get turnips? Shall I eat you up? Shall I gobble you down?

"Gobble, gobble," said the Puff Monster, and he ate up Manya. The Puff Monster grew to three times his normal size.

The children's parents came home and found that the children were gone. Manya and Vanya's mother went to the cellar in search of the children.

The Puff Monster came out of his dark corner. "I am the Puff Monster," he said. "Are you Mother who has come for Manya, who came for Vanya, who came to get some turnips? Shall I eat you up? Shall I gobble you down?

"Gobble, gobble," said the Puff Monster, and he ate up Mother. Now the Puff Monster was four times his normal size.

Finally, Father went to the cellar to see what had happened to Mother.

The Puff Monster came out of his dark corner. "Are you Father who has come for Mother, who came for Manya, who came for Vanya, who came for some turnips? Shall I eat you up? Shall I gobble you down?

"Gobble, gobble," said the Puff Monster, and he ate up Father.

The Puff Monster had gobbled up so many people that he had grown to be enormous. After eating Father, he became five times his normal size. The Puff Monster stretched and stretched. Suddenly, he split open.

Everyone came tumbling out of the Puff Monster—Vanya, Manya, Mother, and Father. From that day on the family went to the cellar without fear, for the Puff Monster was gone forever.

THE ENCHANTED PRINCESS

In a faraway kingdom a soldier served in the Guards. The soldier served faithfully and loyally for twenty-five years, which was the amount of time a peasant was required to serve in the military. For his service, the king ordered that he be discharged. As a reward, he was given the horse he rode while serving in his regiment, as well as its harness and saddle.

The soldier bade his comrades farewell and set out for his native land. He rode one day, two days, three days. Eventually, an entire week went by, then a second, and a third week. The soldier had no more money, and he had nothing with which to feed himself or his horse. Home was still far, far away. He was very hungry, indeed, and he realized that he was in serious trouble.

Looking around, the soldier noticed a large castle. "Well, I might as well go there," he said. "Maybe they'll let me serve for a while so that I can earn some money."

The soldier rode in the direction of the castle. After he entered the courtyard, he tethered his horse and fed it. Only then did he go into the castle. Inside the castle a table was set. Wine and food, whatever the heart desired, was on the table. The soldier ate and drank his fill. "Now," he thought, "I can take a nap."

Suddenly, a bear entered the chamber. "Don't be afraid of me, kind lad. It is good that you came here," the bear said. "I am not a vicious bear, but a beautiful maiden, an enchanted princess. If you spend three nights here and stand your ground, then the spell placed on me will be broken. I will become a princess again, and I will marry you."

The soldier agreed to stay. The bear left, and the soldier remained alone. Such a deep melancholy fell on him that the soldier felt he could not face the world. With the passage of time, his melancholy became even deeper.

On the third day, the soldier's melancholy grew so burdensome that he decided to abandon his plans and run out of the castle. However, no matter how hard he tried or how hard he beat the walls, he could not find an exit. He had no choice but to stay. So he spent the third night in the castle.

In the morning a princess of indescribable beauty appeared before him. She thanked him for the good turn he had done her and ordered that preparations be made for their wedding. They were married and began living together without having a sorrow in the world.

The Enchanted Princess

After some time had passed, the soldier began thinking about his native land. He wanted to go back there.

The princess tried to dissuade him. "Stay here, dear. Don't leave. Don't you have everything you need right here?"

But however hard she tried, she could not dissuade her husband. He was determined to go. Reluctantly, the princess said good-bye. Before he left, she gave her husband a sack full of seeds.

"Whichever road you travel, throw some seeds on both sides of the road," she said. "As soon as the seeds hit the ground, trees will grow from them. The trees will be decorated with expensive fruits. Birds will sing songs on their boughs, and exotic cats from over the seas will tell fairy tales beneath the trees."

The good lad mounted his horse and set out down the road. Wherever he went, he threw seeds on both sides of the road. Forests arose behind him, as if they had crawled out of Damp Mother Earth.*

The soldier rode on for a day, then another, and yet another. On the third day, he came upon a caravan standing in an open field. Not far from the caravan, merchants were sitting on the grass playing cards. Beside them, a kettle was hanging. Although there was no fire beneath the kettle, a broth was bubbling over.

"What a miracle!" the soldier thought. "No fire is visible, yet a broth is bubbling in the kettle. Let's have a closer look."

He turned his horse in the direction of the kettle and approached the merchants. "Hello, honorable gentlemen!"

It never occurred to him that these were not merchants, but in reality devils. "A nice trick you are playing—a kettle boiling without a fire under it! But I have a better trick."

He took a single grain out of his sack and threw it onto the ground. At that moment, there sprung up on the spot a centuries-old tree, adorned with precious fruits and singing birds. And exotic cats from over the seas were telling fairy tales beneath it.

The devils recognized him immediately. "Aha," they said, "he is the one who saved the princess. Because he did so, let's give him a potion, brothers, that will make him sleep for half a year."

The devils began regaling the soldier with food and drink, and then they gave him the magic sleeping potion. Immediately, the soldier fell onto the grass and went into a deep sleep. The merchants, the caravan, and the kettle disappeared.

Soon afterward, the princess went to the garden to take a stroll. She looked up and saw that the tops of the trees had withered. "This is not good," she thought. "Apparently, something bad has happened to my husband. Three months have passed. It is time that he returned, yet he isn't here."

---

*Damp Mother Earth is a pagan deity and nature spirit.

Part 2: Fairy Tales

When her husband failed to return, the princess prepared to go in search of him. She rode down the same road the soldier had taken. Forests were growing on both sides. Birds were singing, and exotic cats from over the seas were meowing fairy tales.

She came to a spot where trees were no longer growing. The road wound through an open field. "Where is he?" she thought. "He couldn't have fallen through the earth!"

Then she saw one of the miraculous trees standing alone. Her dear husband was lying beneath it.

She ran up to him and pushed him in an attempt to waken him, but he did not respond. She began pinching him. She poked his sides with pins. She poked and poked, but he felt no pain. He lay as if dead, without stirring.

The princess grew angry. In a fit of temper, she uttered a curse. "May the wild wind grab you, you sleeping good-for-nothing, and carry you off to unknown lands."

No sooner had she uttered the words, than suddenly winds began whistling and roaring. In a moment the soldier was seized by a wild wind and was borne away from the princess's gaze.

Now the princess thought better of the words she had spoken, but it was too late. Weeping bitter tears, she returned home. There, she began living a lonely existence.

Meanwhile, the poor soldier was carried far away. He was borne beyond three times nine lands into the thirtieth kingdom at the end of the world, where he was thrown down onto a spit between two seas. He fell onto the narrowest wedge. If he had turned either to the right or to the left in his sleep, he would have fallen right into the sea.

The good lad slept half a year without moving a finger. When he awoke, he jumped up and looked around. Waves were breaking on either side, and he could see no end to the broad sea. Standing in perplexity, he asked, "By what miracle did I come here? Who dragged me here?"

He walked along the spit and came to an island. On that island was a high, steep mountain with a summit that rose to the clouds. A large stone was lying on the mountain.

The soldier approached the mountain and came upon three devils fighting so fiercely that pieces of cloth and hair were flying in all directions.

"Stop that! Why are you fighting?" he asked.

"Our father died three days ago, you see. He left three wondrous things—a flying carpet, fast-running boots, and a cap of invisibility. We can't agree on how to divide our inheritance."

"Oh, for goodness sake, how ridiculous it is to fight over such nonsense. Would you like me to divide the inheritance? Everyone will be satisfied, and no one will be offended," said the soldier.

"Please do divide our inheritance for us, fellow countryman," the devils replied.

"All right. Run quickly to the pine forest and collect 100 *poods*, which is equal to 3,600 pounds, of pine pitch and bring it here."

The devils rushed to the pine forest, collected three times that amount of pitch and brought it to the soldier.

"Now go fetch the biggest cauldron you can find in Hell," said the soldier.

The devils went down to Hell and dragged back a very large cauldron, indeed; it held forty barrels of liquid. They put the pitch into the cauldron.

The soldier made a fire and placed the cauldron over it. As soon as the pine pitch melted, he ordered the devils to drag the cauldron up the mountain and to pour hot pine pitch down the mountain. In the blink of an eye, the devils fulfilled the command.

"Now," said the soldier, "give that stone a shove so that it rolls off the mountain. Then, all three of you must chase the stone. Whoever catches up to it first may choose any of the three miraculous objects. Whoever is second to reach the stone gets second choice. The third and last miraculous object belongs to whoever gets there last.

The devils shoved the stone off the mountain. It rolled stiffly down the mountain-side. All three devils gave chase. One of the devils reached the stone and grabbed hold of it. The stone immediately rolled back onto him and pushed him onto the pitch. The second devil caught up, and the third. The same thing happened to them. They all stuck ever so fast to the pitch.

The soldier donned the fast-running boots and placed the cap of invisibility under his arm. Then, he sat on the flying carpet and flew off in search of his own kingdom.

Whether he flew a long or a short time is not known, but eventually he came to a hut on chicken legs. He entered the hut. There sat Baba Yaga, the old, toothless, bony-legged Russian witch.

"Hello, grandma. Tell me what to do. How should I search for my beautiful princess?" the soldier asked.

"I don't know, my dear. I have never seen, nor heard of her. You must travel beyond many seas and beyond many lands to the land where my middle sister lives. She knows more than I do. Perhaps she will be able to tell you."

The soldier sat on the flying carpet and flew off. He traveled around the world. If he wanted to eat or drink, he put on the cap of invisibility and alighted in a town. He went into the shops and took whatever he needed. Then, he flew away on his flying carpet.

Eventually, the soldier came to a second hut on chicken legs. There sat a second Baba Yaga, old, toothless, and bony-legged like her sister. "Hello, grandma, do you know where I might find my beautiful princess?" asked the soldier.

"No, my dear, I don't know. Travel beyond many seas and many lands to the land where my older sister lives. Perhaps she knows."

"Oh, silly woman! You have lived so many years that all your teeth have fallen out, yet you know nothing of any use to me," he said.

The soldier mounted the flying carpet and flew off to Baba Yaga's older sister. He wandered for a long time. He saw many lands and many seas. Finally, he flew to the end of the world. At the end of the world stood a hut on chicken legs, but there was no road beyond the hut. There was only pitch-black darkness so that nothing could be seen. "Well," thought the soldier, "if I can't get any sense out of anyone here, there's nowhere left to fly."

He entered the hut. There sat a third Baba Yaga—old, toothless, and bony-legged like the others. "Hello, grandma! Tell me where to search for my princess."

"Wait a second, and I'll call on the winds and ask them. They blow all over the world, so they must know where your princess is living."

The old woman went onto the porch. She cried in a loud voice and whistled a surprisingly youthful whistle. Wild winds arose and blew in from all directions. The hut shook. "Quiet, quiet!" shouted Baba Yaga.

As soon as the winds had gathered, she said, "My dear wild winds, you blow around the whole wide world. Have you seen the soldier's beautiful princess anywhere?"

"No, we haven't seen her," the winds answered in one voice.

"Is everyone present?"

"Everyone, except the South Wind."

The South Wind came flying up a little later. "Where have you been?" the old woman asked. "We have been waiting for you."

"I'm not to blame, grandma. I visited a new kingdom where a beautiful princess lives. Her husband disappeared without a trace, so now tsars and tsareviches, kings and princes, are courting her.

"Is it far to this new kingdom?"

"It is thirty years distant if one goes on foot. It would take ten years to fly there. But I blow there in three hours."

The soldier asked the South Wind to take him to the new kingdom.

"I will take you there, if you please," said the South Wind. "Just give me permission to go on a spree for three days and three nights after we arrive in your kingdom."

"Go on a spree for three weeks, if you like!"

"Very well, then, I will rest for a day or two to gather my strength. Then, we'll set out."

The South Wind rested. When it had gathered its strength, it said to the soldier, "Well, brother, get ready. Let's set out right away. Don't be afraid. You'll get there in one piece."

Suddenly, a strong whirlwind began blowing and whistling. It grabbed the soldier up into the air and bore him into the clouds, over mountains and seas. After exactly three hours had passed, he was in the kingdom where his beautiful princess lived.

"Good-bye, good lad," the South Wind said. "I have taken pity on you. I don't want to go on a spree in your kingdom."

"Why not?"

"Because if I had gone on a spree, not one house in town, not one tree in the gardens would have remained standing. I would have turned everything topsy-turvy."

"Well, good-bye then. Thank you!" said the soldier. He put on the cap of invisibility and walked toward the white-stoned palace.

While the soldier had been gone, the trees in the gardens stood as if dead, with dry leaves. As soon as he entered the palace, they came to life and began blooming.

The soldier entered a large room. Tsars and tsareviches, kings and princes, were sitting at a table. They had come to court the beautiful princess. They sat drinking sweet wines. Whenever a suitor poured a glass of wine and held it to his lips, the soldier would hit the glass with his fist so that it broke. The guests were amazed. But the beautiful princess guessed right away what was happening. "My dear husband must have returned," she thought.

She looked out the window into the garden and saw that the tops of the trees were blooming. She posed a riddle to her guests. "I had a golden thread and a golden needle. I lost the needle and had not hoped to find it. Now I have found the needle. Whoever can answer the riddle will be my husband."

The tsars and tsareviches, kings and princes, racked their wise brains for a long time, but they could not answer the riddle.

The princess said, "Show yourself, my dear husband."

The soldier took off the cap of invisibility. He took the princess's white hands in his and kissed her sweet lips.

"Here is your answer," said the beautiful princess. "I am the golden thread. My faithful husband is the golden needle. Wherever the needle goes, the thread follows."

So, the suitors had no choice but to go home. They set out in different directions for their courts. The princess and her soldier husband lived happily ever after, enjoying wealth and harmony.

AT THE PIKE'S COMMAND

The massive Russian clay stove (or pec'*) was a focal point of the peasant cottage. It played a significant role as a source of warmth, nourishment, and family social life. It retained its warmth for a long time. Food for both humans and animals was prepared in it. The young, the old, and the sick enjoyed the privilege of sleeping on its warm shelf while the rest of the family slept on benches or on the floor. Lazy Emelia, the hero of this story, selects the stove as the most desirable and comfortable place to ensconce himself.*

Note: You can see a picture of a Russian stove in the color plate section.

There once lived an old man. He had three sons. Two sons were clever, but the youngest, Emelia, was a fool. The clever brothers worked hard, but Emelia lolled on the stove all day long, not caring to do anything or to know anything. The clever brothers had wives, but Emelia had no one.

One day the brothers went off to market. Their wives began sending Emelia on errands. "Emelia, go fetch some water!"

"I don't want to," Emelia groaned from his warm bed atop the stove.

"Do it, Emelia, or else when your brothers return from market they won't bring you any presents."

"Well, all right, then," Emelia replied. He climbed down from the stove. He put on his shoes, got dressed, took two buckets and an ax, and set out for the river.

He chopped a hole in the ice and scooped up some water with the buckets. He set the buckets down and stared into the hole in the ice. Emelia spied a pike in the hole. He managed to catch the pike with his bare hands.

"The pike will make a tasty fish soup," he thought.

Suddenly, the pike spoke to him in a human voice. "Emelia, set me free. Throw me back into the water, and one day I will be of use to you."

Emelia just laughed. "How could you be of any use to me? No, I'm taking you home. I'll have my sisters-in-law make fish soup with you. The soup will taste good."

Once again, the pike begged, "Emelia, Emelia, set me free. Throw me back into the water, and I'll do anything you wish."

"Very well, then, but first prove to me that you aren't deceiving me. Then I'll let you go."

"Emelia, Emelia, just tell me what you are wishing this very moment," the pike said.

"I am wishing that the buckets would go home of their own accord without any water splashing out of them."

"Remember my words," the pike said. "When you want something, you have only to say, 'At the pike's command, and by my desire.'"

Emelia repeated, "At the pike's command, and by my desire, take yourselves home, buckets."

No sooner had he uttered these words than the buckets started going up the hill by themselves. Emelia released the pike into the hole in the ice, and he followed the buckets back to the house.

As the buckets went through the village, the people stared, amazed at the sight. Emelia walked behind the buckets chuckling. The buckets went into the cottage and placed themselves on a bench. Emelia climbed back up onto the stove.

After some time had passed, his sisters-in-law said, "Emelia, why are you lolling about? Go chop some wood."

"I don't want to," Emelia groaned.

"If you don't chop some wood, your brothers won't bring any gifts for you when they return home from market."

Emelia did not want to climb down from the stove. He remembered the pike and said quietly, "At the pike's command, and by my desire, go chop wood, ax. And wood, bring yourself into the cottage and put yourself into the stove."

The ax jumped up from under the bench. It went into the yard and began chopping wood. The wood went into the cottage and climbed into the stove on its own.

After some more time had passed, the sisters-in-law said once again, "Emelia, we have no more wood. Go to the forest and chop down some trees."

"What on earth for?" Emelia asked from atop the stove.

"What do you mean—'What on earth for'? Is it our work to go to the forest for wood?"

"I don't want to," groaned Emelia.

"Well, then, there won't be any gifts for you."

It could not be helped. Emelia climbed down from the stove. He put on his shoes and got dressed. Taking a rope and an ax, he went into the yard and got into the sleigh. "Women, open the gate!" he commanded.

"What are you doing, fool?" his sisters-in-law asked. "You have seated yourself in the sleigh without harnessing the horses to it."

"I don't need horses."

The sisters-in-law opened the gate.

"At the pike's command, and by my desire, go into the forest, sleigh," Emelia said quietly.

The sleigh went through the gate by itself, and so quickly that horses could not have caught up with it.

To get to the forest, Emelia had to ride through town. In the process, he trampled and hit many people. "Hold him!" people shouted. "Catch him!" But Emelia paid no attention; he simply urged the sleigh onward.

When Emelia came to the forest, he said, "At the pike's command, and by my desire, chop some dry wood, ax. And wood, you stack yourselves up in the sleigh and tie yourselves to it."

The ax began chopping away. It chopped down some dry trees, and the wood stacked itself up in the sleigh and bound itself with a rope.

Then Emelia asked the ax to make a club for himself, so large that it would be difficult to raise it. He sat down on top of the load of wood and said, "At the pike's command, and by my desire, go home, sleigh."

The sleigh dashed home. Once again Emelia rode through town, where recently he had trampled and hit many people. Angered, they were waiting for him. They grabbed Emelia, dragged him off the wagon, and scolded and beat him.

He saw that it was bad business, but he remembered his club. "At the pike's command, and by my desire, strike out on all sides, club," he said quietly.

The club hopped up and began battering everyone. People rushed away in all directions. Emelia went home and crawled back onto the stove.

Sooner or later, the tsar heard about Emelia's antics and sent an officer to fetch him—to find him and bring him to the palace.

The officer came to the village and entered the cottage where Emelila lived. "Are you Emelia the Fool?"

"What's it to you?" Emelia asked from atop the stove.

"Get dressed quickly. I'm taking you to the tsar."

"I don't want to go," groaned Emelia.

The officer got angry and slapped Emelia on the cheek.

"Club," Emelia said quietly, "at the pike's command, and by my desire, hit every part of his body."

The club sprang to action. It struck the officer so hard that he ran away only with difficulty.

The tsar was amazed that his officer could not manage Emelia. This time he sent his greatest grandee. "Bring Emelia the Fool to my palace, or I'll chop off your head," said the tsar.

The very great grandee bought raisins, plums, and honey cakes. When he arrived in the village, he entered the cottage and asked the sisters-in-law what Emelia was fond of.

"Our Emelia likes it when people ask him for favors affectionately and when they promise him a red caftan.* Then, he'll do anything they ask of him."

The very great grandee gave Emelia the raisins, plums, and honey cakes. Then, he said, "Emelia, Emelia, why are you lolling on the stove? Let's go to the tsar."

"I am warm here."

"Emelia, Emelia, the tsar will give you food and drink. Please, let's go!"

"I don't want to."

"Emelia, Emelia, the tsar will give you a red caftan, a cap, and boots."

Emelia gave the grandee's comments some thought, then said, "Well, all right. You go ahead, and I'll follow you."

The grandee left. Emelia kept lying where he was while saying, "At the pike's command, and by my desire, go to the tsar, stove."

The corners of the cottage began splitting. The roof began to sway. The walls flew apart, and the stove began going down the road on its own. It was headed straight for the tsar's.

The tsar looked out the window and marveled, "What wonder is this?"

The very great grandee answered, "That is Emelia coming to see you on his stove."

The tsar went onto the porch. "Emelia, I have complaints against you. You have trampled many people."

"Then why did they crawl under the sleigh?"

At that moment, the tsar's daughter, Tsarevna Mar'ia, looked out the window at Emelia.

Emelia saw her looking out the window and said quietly, "At the pike's command, and by my desire, may the tsar's daughter fall in love with me."

Then, he said, "Take me home, stove."

The stove turned around and went home. It entered the cottage and stood in its previous place. Once again, Emelia lolled about on top of it.

Meanwhile, in the tsar's palace, there were screams and tears. Tsarevna Mar'ia missed Emelia, and she said she could not live without him. She asked her father to give her hand in marriage to Emelia.

The tsar grieved and spoke again to his very great grandee. "Go bring Emelila to me, dead or alive, or else I'll chop off your head," he said.

The very great grandee bought sweet wine and tasty hors d'oeuvres (*zakuski*). He went to the village, entered the cottage, and began treating Emelia to the goodies he had brought.

Emelia ate and drank his fill. He got tipsy and lay down to sleep. Then the grandee put him into his carriage and brought him to the tsar.

---

*A long robe or coat.

Immediately, the tsar ordered that a big barrel with iron hoops be brought. Emelia and Tsarevna Mar'ia were placed in it. Then, the barrel was tarred and thrown into the sea.

After a long or short time, Emelia awoke. He noticed that it was dark and cramped. "Where am I?" he asked.

A voice answered. "It's boring and tedious here, Emeliushka.* They tarred us into this barrel and threw us into the blue sea."

"And who are you?"

"I am Tsarevna Mar'ia."

"At the pike's command, and by my desire, roll the barrel onto the dry shore, wild winds. Roll it onto the yellow sand," said Emelia.

The wild winds blew. The sea became agitated. The barrel was thrown onto the dry shore, onto the yellow sand. Emelia and Tsarevna Mar'ia got out.

"Emeliushka, where will we live? Build a little cottage for us."

"I don't want to," Emelia said.

Tsarevna Mar'ia began begging even harder.

Finally, Emelia said, "At the pike's command, and by my desire, build a palace made of white stone with a golden roof."

He had no sooner uttered the words than a palace constructed of white stone with a golden roof appeared. A green garden with blooming flowers and singing birds surrounded the palace. Tsarevna Mar'ia and Emelia went into the palace and sat near a window.

"Emeliushka, can't you become handsome?" asked Tsarevna Mar'ia.

Emelia gave little thought to it before saying, "At the pike's command, and by my desire, make me a fine young man who is indescribably good looking."

Emelia became more handsome than any story could tell or any pen could describe.

At that moment the tsar was hunting. While hunting, he came upon a palace where there had never been one before. "Who built a palace on my land without my permission? What lout did this?" he asked.

The tsar sent one of his men to find out who lived there. His emissaries ran up to the palace. They stood beneath a window and asked who lived there.

"Ask the tsar to visit me, and I'll tell him myself," Emelia said.

The tsar came to visit. Emelia met him and led him into the palace. He invited him to sit at the table. They began feasting together.

The tsar ate and drank and did not cease being amazed. "Who are you, fine lad?"

"Do you remember Emelia the Fool who came to visit you on a stove and whom you ordered to be tarred into a barrel with your daughter and thrown into the sea? Well, I am that Emelia. If I want, I can burn down and destroy your entire kingdom."

---

*The diminutive form of Emelia.

The tsar took fright and began begging Emelia's pardon. "Marry my daughter, Emeliushka. Take my kingdom. Just don't destroy me."

A feast was held to which the entire kingdom was invited. Emelia married Tsarevna Mar'ia and began ruling the kingdom.

This is the end of the tale. Whoever listens to it is a fine fellow.

THE SUN, THE MOON, AND RAVEN VORONOVICH

Once upon a time, there lived an old woman and an old man. The couple had three daughters of marriageable age who were very dear to them.

One day the old man went to the barn to get some grain. He poured the grain into a sack and began carrying the sack home. He failed to notice that there was a hole in the sack, so little by little the grain fell out of the sack onto the pathway.

When the old man arrived home, his wife asked, "Where is the grain?"

"It must have fallen out on the way home," the old man replied.

"Go gather it up," the old woman ordered.

The old man retraced his steps. He picked and picked at the tiny kernels of grain until it grew dark and he was very tired. "Oh," he moaned, "if only the Sun would shine and the Moon would glow and Raven Voronovich would help me gather the spilled grain! In return I would give them my daughters in marriage. I would give my oldest daughter to the Sun, my middle daughter to the Moon, and my youngest daughter to Raven Voronovich."

No sooner had the old man uttered these words than night became day and the Sun began shining. Raven Voronovich flew up and worked all day long gathering grain. At night the Moon began glowing, and Raven Voronovich continued gathering all the grain down to the last kernel.

When the old man returned home, he said to his oldest daughter, "Put on your best dress and go out onto the porch. Your bridegroom is waiting for you."

The oldest daughter dressed up and stepped out onto the porch. The Sun, who was waiting for her, carried her away.

The old man ordered his middle daughter to put on her best dress and go out onto the porch. The Moon grabbed her and took her away.

Then, the old man ordered his youngest daughter to do the same. Raven Voronovich grabbed her and spirited her away, too.

After their daughters had gone, the old people grew lonely. One day the old man said, "I miss my daughters. I think I'll go visit them." And he set out.

He walked on and on until he had worn out his birch-bark shoes. Finally, he came to the home of the fiery Sun.

The Sun and his wife greeted him. "Father, how can we entertain you?" they asked.

"Well, I would like to eat some pancakes. I'm hungry," the old man replied.

"Then pancakes it will be," said the Sun. "Mix the dough, wife."

The old man's oldest daughter mixed the dough. Then, the Sun sat down on the floor and said, "Well, wife, start cooking the pancakes."

The Sun's wife put a frying pan on the Sun's head and cooked the pancakes.

The old man was amazed. After he had eaten his fill, he went home. There, he ordered the old woman to prepare some pancake dough.

The old woman mixed the dough and went to light the stove, but the old man would not allow it. He sat down on the floor and ordered his wife to put the frying pan on his bald spot.

"The pancakes won't cook on your head," the old woman protested.

"Yes, they will. You'll see," the old man insisted.

It could not be helped. The old woman obeyed. She put the frying pan on the old man's head. The frying pan sat there all day long, but the pancakes did not cook up.

Finally, the old woman lit the stove and grumbled as she cooked the pancakes the usual way. Her husband said not a word and ate his fill.

The next day, the old man set out to visit his middle daughter. He walked on and on until he arrived at the home of the bright Moon.

The Moon and his wife greeted him happily. They, too, asked, "How can we entertain you, Father?"

"I am full," the old man said, "but I would like to steam away the dirt from my journey in the bathhouse."

"The bathhouse will be ready in a moment, Father."

After the bathhouse had been heated, the Moon led the old man into it and said, "Well, Father, wash and steam to your heart's content."

"It's dark in here," the old man complained.

"Just a minute," the Moon replied. "I'll fix that. It will be light in a moment." He stuck his finger into a chink in the wall, and a light began glowing inside the bathhouse.

The old man steamed to his satisfaction. Then, he went home.

As soon as it got dark, he sent the old woman out to heat up the bathhouse. "But can't you see that it's dark out? How can we steam ourselves in the dark?"

"It's all right. There will be light."

The old woman heated the bathhouse and said, "Go on in."

"No," replied the old man, "you go first. I'll give you a light."

The old woman went into the bathhouse. The old man had observed how the Moon had given him a light, and he did the same for the old woman. He stuck his finger into a chink in the wall and asked, "Is it light now?"

"It's as dark as if someone had poked out my eye," the old woman answered.

The old woman began grumbling. She got a lantern and went back into the bathhouse to wash up.

The next day, the old man said, "Well, now I'll go visit my youngest daughter." He set out.

When he arrived at the home of Raven Voronovich, his youngest daughter was very happy to see him, as was her husband.

They did not know where to put the old man or how to entertain him. When they asked what they could do for him, the old man said, "You had better put me to bed. I am very tired."

Raven Voronovich led the old man to his roost. He placed a ladder beneath it and said, "Climb up, Father. Now all of us will go to sleep."

The old man climbed up onto the roost. Raven Voronovich put him under one wing, and he put his wife under the other wing. All three fell into a sweet sleep.

In the morning, the old man got ready to go home.

"Why are you leaving so soon?" asked Raven Voronovich.

"It's time for me to go. The old woman is probably tired of waiting for me."

The old man returned home. When evening came the old woman started making the bed. Her husband would not allow it. "We'll sleep on the roost tonight with the chickens," he announced.

This time the old woman lost her patience. "You sleep on the chicken roost if you want, but our bed is just fine for me!"

The old man went to the hen coop, climbed up onto the roost with the hens, and dozed off.

No sooner had he fallen asleep than he fell—kerplunk—off the roost. He got a lump on his forehead, tore his shirt and pants, and frightened the chickens almost to death.

The foolish old man picked himself up off the floor of the hen coop. Moaning and groaning, he trudged back to the cottage to sleep in his own bed. He climbed into bed quietly so that he would not awaken the old woman.

PART 3

TALES OF EVERYDAY LIFE

THE EGG

There once lived an old woman and an old man. They had a hen named Speckles. One day Speckles laid an egg under the floor. The egg was beautiful. It was multicolored, bright, and smooth as ivory. It was a very unique egg, indeed.

The old couple found the egg. The old man inspected it. He hit the egg, and wonder of wonders—the egg did not break. The old woman hit the egg, too, but it did not break. Then, a little mouse ran by and in so doing flicked its tail against the egg. The egg rolled onto the floor and broke into smithereens.

The old man cried, and the old woman wept. Grief-stricken, Speckles the hen cackled. As if sympathizing with them, the gate squeaked and the shingles came loose on the cottage roof and flew into the air.

The priest's daughters, who were passing on their way to the village well to fetch water, asked the old couple, "Why are you crying?"

"Why wouldn't we cry?" the old woman answered. "We have a hen named Speckles. She laid an egg under the floor. The egg was multicolored, bright, and smooth as ivory. It was a very unique egg, indeed. The old man hit it, and it didn't break. I hit it, and it didn't break. Then, a little mouse ran up to the egg and flicked its tail. The egg rolled onto the floor and broke into pieces."

After the priest's daughters heard what had happened, they threw their buckets to the ground, broke the yokes used for carrying the buckets, and returned home empty-handed, so grief-stricken were they.

"Oh, Mother," they said to the priest's wife, "you have no idea what is going on in the world. An old woman and an old man have a hen named Speckles. She laid an egg under the floor. The egg was multicolored, bright, and smooth as ivory. It was a very unique egg, indeed. The old man hit it, and it didn't break. The old woman hit it, and it didn't break. Then, a little mouse ran up to the egg and flicked its tail. The egg rolled onto the floor and broke into pieces. Now the old man is crying and the old woman is weeping. Speckles the Hen is cackling. The gate squeaked in sympathy, and the shingles came loose from the cottage roof and flew into the air. We were on our way to the village well to fetch water when we heard about the great misfortune. We threw down our buckets and broke the yoke used for carrying the buckets."

At that moment the priest's wife was kneading dough. When she heard that the old man was crying, the old woman was weeping, and that Speckles the Hen was cackling, she overturned the dough trough and the dough dropped onto the floor.

The priest came through the cottage door with a book.

"Oh, little Father," the priest's wife said to him, "you know nothing of what goes on in the world. An old woman and an old man have a hen named Speckles. She laid an egg under the floor. The egg was multicolored, bright, and smooth as ivory. It was a very unique egg, indeed. The old man hit it, and it didn't break. The old woman hit it, and it didn't break. Then, a little mouse ran up to the egg and flicked its tail. The egg rolled to the floor and broke into pieces. Now the old man is crying, and the old woman is weeping. Speckles the Hen is cackling. The gate squeaked in sympathy, and the shingles came loose from the cottage roof and flew into the air. Our daughters, who were on their way to the village well to fetch water, threw down their buckets and broke the yokes used for carrying the buckets. I was kneading dough, and because of my great sorrow, I dropped the dough onto the floor."

The priest, too, grieved and sorrowed. In his grief, he tore his book to shreds. All of these misfortunes were caused by one little egg.

A COPECK A DROP

A hungry soldier went to a cottage where a greedy woman lived. "Please feed me with whatever God has given you, whatever you have," he said to the woman.

"With pleasure, soldier," said the woman. "But don't take offense. The only food I have is plain cabbage soup (*shchi*)."

"What do you mean by 'plain' cabbage soup?"

"The soup has only cabbage in it and nothing else."

"Isn't there any oil in it?"

"Of course not, soldier. Oil is very expensive."

"How expensive?"

"It costs a copeck* a drop."

"All right," said the soldier. "Give me some oil, and I'll pay for it."

The old woman ladled out a bowl of cabbage soup. She took a pot of heated oil from the stove and dribbled one tiny drop into the bowl. The golden drop sparkled in the soup.

"Give me another," said the soldier.

The woman dribbled another drop into the cabbage soup. The second golden drop sparkled in the soup.

"Give me another," the soldier said.

The woman dribbled yet another tiny drop into the cabbage soup.

It was not enough for the soldier. He took the pot out of the woman's hand and splashed its entire contents into the bowl of soup.

*At one time comparable to our penny. There are 100 copecks in a ruble. The ruble is Russia's basic monetary unit.

Five, ten, twenty—a countless number of golden droplets began sparkling in the cabbage soup. Suddenly, they merged into one large drop.

"I see only one drop in the soup," the soldier said to the woman.

He gave the stingy woman a single copeck for the large drop of oil and ate his soup in peace.

MAGIC WATER

There once lived a husband and a wife. In their youth, they had lived in harmony. However, in old age it was as if someone had substituted them for a completely different quarrelsome old couple.

In the morning, no sooner would the old man dangle his legs down from the shelf above the stove, where he slept, than a squabble would break out between him and his old wife. He would say a word to the old woman, and she would reply with two words. He would say two words, and she would reply with five words. He would utter five words, and the old woman would retort with ten words. And so it went. It was as if a whirlwind were spinning round between them. Anyone who heard them wanted to run out of the house as soon as possible.

When they began trying to figure out who was to blame for the discord, it appeared that either no one was at fault or the other one was at fault.

"Why are we like this, old woman?" the old man would ask.

"It's all your fault, old man. It's all you!" the old woman would reply.

"Enough! So, it's me? What about you with your long tongue?"

"It's not me. It's you!"

"No, it's you, not me!"

And they would start going at it again.

A neighbor listened to the couple quarreling daily until she grew quite tired of hearing them. She offered a suggestion. "Maremianushka," she said, for Maremianushka was the old woman's name, "why don't you get along with your husband? You should go to the witch who lives on the outskirts of the village. She'll chant over a healing potion for you. She helps people, and who knows, she may be able to help you."

"She's right," thought the old woman. "I'll go to the witch."

When she came to the witch's cottage, she knocked on the window. The witch came out. "What do you want, old woman?" the witch asked.

"Here's the situation," Maremianushka answered. "My old man and I fight all the time."

"Wait a moment," the witch said, and she went back into her cottage. She brought out some water in a wooden ladle and whispered a spell over it. Then, she poured the water into a glass vessel and gave it to Maremianushka.

"After you arrive home," the witch said, "whenever your old man starts making a fuss, take a spoonful of water. Don't spit it out or swallow it. Just hold it in your mouth until he calms down, and everything will be fine."

Maremianushka bowed to the witch and took the vessel of water home.

She had no sooner crossed the threshold of her home than the old man flew at her.

"Oh, you women are chatterboxes! A man comes home, and it's as if his wife has disappeared. The tea should have been brewed long ago, but you have forgotten it. And where did you vanish to?"

Maremianushka took a spoonful of water from the glass vessel. She did as the witch had commanded. She neither spit it out, nor swallowed it. Rather, she held it in her mouth.

The old man, noticing that his wife did not answer, grew silent too. The old woman was happy. "It's plain to see that this is magic healing water," she thought.

She set down the vessel of water and busied herself setting up the samovar* to make tea. The chimney of the samovar rattled as she placed it into the center.

The old man heard the noise she was making and said, "What a clumsy paws! You're sticking the wrong end of the chimney into the samovar."

The old woman wanted to give him a smart answer back, but she remembered the witch's instructions. Again, she took a spoonful of water. She held the water in her mouth.

The old man noticed that the old woman was not uttering a single contrary word. He was amazed, and he too grew silent.

From that day on, everything went perfectly. Once again, the old couple lived in harmony as they had when they were young. People thought that they were a lovely sight together. Whenever the old man started making a fuss, Maremianushka went straight for the magic water. Such was the water's power!

---

*A metal urn used to heat water for brewing tea.

THE DEVIL LOANS MONEY

A farmer fell on bad times. To get out of his situation, he needed money. But he had none. "Where can I get some money?" he asked himself. Finally, he came up with the idea of going to the devil and asking him for a loan.

He went to the devil and said, "Devil, how about giving me a loan?"

"Why do you want a loan?" asked the devil.

"To get out of debt," the farmer replied.

"How much do you want?"

"A thousand rubles."*

"When do you have to pay off your debt?"

"Tomorrow."

"I'll give you the money with pleasure," said the devil, and he counted out a thousand rubles. "But remember," he warned, "that you must give back both the money and your soul as well for interest."

The next day the devil came to the farmer's home to collect what the man owed.

"Come back tomorrow," the farmer told him.

The day after, the devil came to the farmer to collect the debt.

"Come back tomorrow," the farmer said once again.

For the third time the devil came to the man to collect the money owed him.

Again, the farmer ordered him to come back the next day. So it went for several days.

One day the farmer said to the devil, "Why should you have to come to me so often. It is a great inconvenience for you. I'll hang a board on my gate, and I'll write on it when you should come to collect the debt."

"All right," the devil agreed, and he left.

The farmer wrote, "Come tomorrow" on a board, and he hung the board on the gate. The devil came once, twice—but the same inscription was always on the board.

---

*Russia's basic monetary unit, once similar in concept to the American dollar.

"Let's see what happens if I don't go tomorrow," the devil thought. The next day he did not bother going to collect his money.

The day afterward he went to the farmer. Another inscription was on the gate. It read: "Come yesterday."

"Oh, dear, I'm done for," thought the devil. "I didn't go to collect my money and the farmer's soul yesterday, so apparently I've lost the opportunity to do so."

The devil decided to forgive the farmer his debt.

RABBIT DREAMS

A poor man was walking through a field when he caught sight of a wild rabbit hiding under a bush.

"Here is my chance to get rich and have my own house to live in," the man said. "I will catch that rabbit and sell him for twelve copecks.*

"With the money I receive from the sale of the rabbit, I'll buy a pig. The pig will give me twelve piglets.

"When the piglets grow up, each piglet will have twelve more piglets. Then, I'll sell them. I'll buy a house with the money so that I can get married.

"My wife will bear me two fine sons, whom I'll call Vaska and Vanka. They will plow the field while I sit on a bench under the window making sure that everything is done right.

" 'Look here, Vaska and Vanka,' I'll shout. 'Don't make the hired hands work so hard. Use a little elbow grease yourselves!' "

In his excitement the man shouted so loud that the rabbit took fright and ran away. Everything else disappeared with the rabbit—the house with all its wealth, the wife, and the two children Vaska and Vanka.

---

*There are 100 copecks in a ruble. At one time a copeck could have been compared to a penny, but today its value is insignificant.

THE SORCERER

There once lived a poor, but crafty, little man by the name of Beetle. One day he stole a piece of canvas from a woman and hid it in a haystack. Then, he began bragging that he was a master sorcerer. The woman from whom he had stolen the canvas came to him and asked him to find out what had happened to the piece of cloth.

"What will you give me for my efforts if I find it?" asked Beetle.

"I'll give you a *pood** of flour and a pound of butter," the woman answered.

"All right!" Beetle agreed.

The sly little man began his psychic reading. He cast a spell and told the woman where the canvas was hidden. Naturally, she was amazed to find it in the haystack, exactly where Beetle had said it would be. She sang Beetle's praises to anyone who would listen. News of Beetle's success spread throughout the village.

After two or three days had passed, the stallion of Beetle's neighbor, a wealthy landowner, disappeared. Beetle had led the stallion into the forest and had tied it to a tree. The landowner sent for the sorcerer.

Beetle cast a spell. "Go to the forest quickly," he said. "You will find the stallion tied to a tree."

It happened just as Beetle had said. The stallion was led out of the forest. The landowner gave Beetle a hundred rubles.† Soon the sorcerer's fame had spread throughout the kingdom.

Shortly thereafter, the tsar's wedding ring disappeared. The tsar searched and searched, but the ring was nowhere to be found. The tsar sent for the sorcerer and asked that he be brought to the palace as soon as possible. Beetle was placed in a carriage and brought to the tsar.

"Now I'm done for," thought Beetle. "How on earth should I know what happened to the tsar's ring?"

"Hello, sorcerer," said the tsar. "Cast your spell for me. If you guess where my ring is, I'll reward you with a great deal of money. If you don't guess correctly, it's off with your head!"

---

*Approximately thirty-six pounds.
†The ruble is Russia's basic monetary unit.

The tsar ordered that the sorcerer be taken to a special room. "Let him cast spells all night long so that he'll be ready with the answer in the morning."

The sorcerer sat in the room and thought, "What answer will I give the tsar? I'd better wait until midnight and run in whatever direction my nose points. When I hear the third cock crowing, I'll run away."

In actuality the tsar's ring had been stolen by three courtiers—the footman, the coachman, and the cook.

"What will we do, brothers?" they asked one another. "If that sorcerer finds out about us, our death is inevitable. Let's eavesdrop at his door. If he doesn't know anything, we'll keep silent. But if he's found us out, then it can't be helped—we'll have to beg him not to inform the tsar."

First the footman eavesdropped at the door.

Suddenly, the cock crowed. Beetle muttered, "There's one. Now I just have to wait for the other two." He meant that one cock's crow had passed and that he had only two more cock's crows to wait for until he made his escape.

The footman did not interpret it that way. After the footman heard Beetle's words, his heart sank to his boots. He ran to his friends. "Oh, brothers," he cried. "He's found me out. As soon as I went up to the door, he cried, 'There's one. Now I just have to wait for the other two.'"

"Wait, I'll go next," said the coachman, and he went to eavesdrop at the door.

The second cock's crow rang out. "There's the second one," said Beetle. "Now I just have to wait for one more."

"Oh, brothers," cried the coachman. "He's found me out too."

"If he's found me out," said the cook, "let's go straight to him. We'll fall to our knees before him and try to dissuade him from telling on us."

The cook went to Beetle's door to eavesdrop.

The third cock's crow rang out. "There's the third one," said Beetle.

Beetle rushed to the door. He wanted to run away. The thieves met him and fell to their knees.

"Don't ruin us," they begged. "Don't tell the tsar. Here's the ring."

"Well, have it your way," said Beetle. "I forgive you."

Beetle took the ring. He lifted the floor covering and threw the ring under it.

In the morning the tsar asked, "Well, my dear man, how did you do? What did you find out?"

"I cast my spells. They revealed that your ring has rolled under the floor covering in my room."

The floor covering was raised, and the ring was found. The tsar rewarded the sorcerer generously and ordered that he be given food and drink until he was stuffed.

Meanwhile, the tsar went to the garden to take a stroll. As he was walking down a garden path, he spied a beetle. He picked it up and returned to the sorcerer.

"If you really are a sorcerer, tell me what I have in my hand," the tsar said.

The sorcerer took fright and said, "Well, you're caught now, Beetle. You've fallen right into the tsar's hands."

"You're right!" declared the amazed tsar. "I've got a beetle in my hands." He rewarded Beetle with more gifts and sent him home with honors and high regard.

THE EXCHANGE

One day, while bathing in the river, a rich merchant fell into a deep hole. Because he did not know how to swim, he began to drown. An old man, an ordinary peasant, heard his cry for help. The old man jumped into the water and pulled out the merchant.

The merchant did not know how to thank the old man. He invited him to visit him in town, where he entertained him royally. In addition, the merchant gave the old man a piece of gold the size of a horse's head as a reward for saving his life.

The little old man took the gold and headed home. On the way he met a horse dealer, who was driving a herd of horses.

"Hello, old man!" said the horse dealer. "Where have you come from?"

"From a rich merchant in town," the old man replied.

"What did the merchant give you?"

"A piece of gold the size of a horse's head."

"Give me the gold, and take my best horse in exchange," said the horse dealer.

The old man selected the best horse. He thanked the horse dealer, and went on.

Next, the old man met a herdsman driving oxen.

"Hello, old man!" said the herdsman. "Where have you come from?"

"From a rich merchant in town."

"What did the merchant give you?"

"A piece of gold the size of a horse's head."

"Where is it?"

"I exchanged it for a horse."

"Exchange the horse for any ox you like," proposed the herdsman.

The old man selected an ox. He thanked the herdsman, and went on.

Then, he met a shepherd driving a flock of sheep.

"Hello, old man!" said the shepherd. "Where have you come from?"

"From a rich merchant in town."

"What did the merchant give you?"

"A piece of gold the size of a horse's head."

"Where is it?"

"I exchanged it for a horse."

"Where is the horse?"

"I exchanged it for an ox."

"Exchange the ox for any ram that takes your fancy," said the shepherd.

The old man selected the best ram. He thanked the shepherd, and went on.

The next person the old man met was a swineherd, who was driving his swine.

"Hello, old man!" said the swineherd. "Where have you come from?"

"From a rich merchant in town."

"What did the merchant give you?"

"A piece of gold the size of a horse's head."

"Where is it?"

"I exchanged it for a horse."

"And where is the horse?"

"I exchanged it for an ox."

"Where is the ox?"

"I exchanged it for a ram."

"Give me the ram, and instead pick out the best piglet," said the swineherd.

The old man selected a piglet. He thanked the swineherd and went on.

Soon afterward the old man met a peddler with a basket on his back.

"Hello, old man!" said the peddler. "Where have you come from?"

"From a rich merchant in town."

"What did the merchant give you?"

"A piece of gold the size of a horse's head."

"Where is it?"

"I exchanged it for a horse."

"Where is the horse?"

"I exchanged it for an ox."

"And where is the ox?"

"I exchanged it for a ram."

"Where is the ram?"

"I exchanged it for a piglet."

"Give me the piglet, and take any needle you like," proposed the peddler.

The old man selected a marvelous needle—shiny, strong, and straight. He thanked the peddler and went on.

Finally, the old man arrived home. Unfortunately, as he was climbing over the wattle fence, he lost the needle.

His old wife came running to meet him. "Oh, my dear, I was completely lost here without you. Well, tell me, were you at the merchant's?"

"I was."

"What did the merchant give you?"

"A piece of gold the size of a horse's head."

"Where is it?"

"I exchanged it for a horse."

"Where is the horse?"

"I exchanged it for an ox."

"And where is the ox?"

"I exchanged it for a ram."

"Where is the ram?"

"I exchanged it for a piglet."

"Where is the piglet?"

"I exchanged it for a needle. I wanted to bring back the needle as a gift for you. But as I was climbing over the wattle fence, I lost the needle."

"It's all right, dear. It's good that you got home safely," said his wife. "Now, come into the cottage and eat your supper."

To this day the old woman and the old man are living together in joy and harmony. They have no need of gold to be happy.

THE FOOL AND THE BIRCH TREE

Once upon a time, in a faraway kingdom, there lived an old man. The old man had three sons. Two of the sons were clever, but the third son was a fool.

When the old man died, the sons divided his estate by casting lots. The clever sons received most of the old man's property, and the fool received only an ox—and a skinny one at that!

When market day came, the clever brothers got ready to go to market to sell their wares.

The fool noticed what they were doing and said, "Brothers, I think I'll go to market, too. I think I'll sell my ox."

The fool hooked a rope around the ox's horns and began leading it to town. On the way to town, he had to pass through a forest. An old, dry birch tree was standing in the forest. The wind was blowing, and the branches of the birch were creaking.

"Why is the birch tree creaking?" wondered the fool. "Perhaps it wants to buy my ox."

"Hey, birch tree, do you want to buy my ox for twenty rubles?"* the fool asked the tree.

The birch tree did not answer. It only creaked all the more. The fool imagined that it was asking to buy the ox on credit.

"All right, then. If you wish, I'll wait until tomorrow for payment. I'll leave the ox here and return for my money tomorrow."

The fool tied the ox to the birch tree. Then, he took his final leave of the ox and went home.

His clever brothers came home and began questioning him. "Well, did you sell your ox, fool?"

"I sold it."

"Did you sell it for a lot of money?"

"I sold it for twenty rubles."

"Where's the money?"

---

*The ruble is Russia's basic monetary unit.

"I haven't received the money yet. I'm supposed to go get it tomorrow."

"Oh, you simpleton!"

The next morning the fool got up, got dressed, and went to the birch tree for his money. He went into the forest. As he approached the birch tree, it was swaying in the wind. The ox was not there because wolves had eaten it during the night.

"Well, neighbor, give me the money. You promised that you would pay up today."

The wind blew, and the birch tree began creaking.

"Get out of here! What a disloyal friend you turned out to be! Yesterday you said, 'I'll give you the money tomorrow.' And now you promise to do the same. Well, let it be as you wish. I'll wait one more day. But I won't wait longer than that. I need the money myself, you know."

The fool returned home. Again, his brothers began badgering him. "Well, did you receive the money?"

"No, brothers, I'm going to have to wait a little longer for the money."

"To whom did you sell the ox?"

"To the dry birch in the forest."

"What an idiot!"

The third day, the fool took an ax and set out for the forest. He approached the tree and demanded his money. The tree just creaked and creaked.

"No, neighbor, if you constantly say 'tomorrow,' then I'll never receive anything from you. I don't like jokes. I'll settle accounts with you quickly!"

The fool grabbed the ax and began chopping so hard that chips of wood scattered in all directions. As it so happened, there was a hollow in the tree where robbers had hidden a kettle full of gold. When the tree split in half, the fool noticed the gold. He gathered as much gold as he could from the bottom of the hollow and carried it home. He showed it to his brothers.

"Where did you get so much money, fool?" they asked.

"The birch tree, my neighbor, gave it to me for my ox. But this is only half of it. I couldn't drag the other half home by myself. Let's go get the rest, brothers."

The brothers went to the forest. They gathered up the rest of the money and carried it home.

Regale me with ale
For telling my tale.

THREE FANCY BREADS AND A PRETZEL

A peasant was hungry, so he bought a fancy bread and ate it. After eating the fancy bread, he was still hungry.

He bought another fancy bread and ate it. But, still he was hungry.

He bought yet another fancy bread and ate it. However, he was still hungry, and his stomach was growling.

Finally, he bought a pretzel. After eating just one pretzel, he was full and satisfied.

The peasant hit his forehead with the palm of his hand and said, "What an idiot I am! Why did I eat so may fancy breads when I had only to eat one pretzel to feel full?"

THE BUBBLE, THE STRAW, AND THE *LAPOT'*

The lapot' *(plural form is* lapti*), or bast shoe, was worn in summer by the Russian peasant. The shoe was woven by the village* lapti *maker from linden tree fibers into a basket weave design. It was a light, inexpensive footwear.*

Note: You can see a picture of *lapti* in the color plate section.

There once lived three friends—a Bubble, a piece of Straw, and a *Lapot'*. It was the friends' custom to journey together. On one of their trips, they came to a river and did not know how to get across.

The *Lapot'* said to the Bubble, "Bubble, let me swim across the river on your back."

"No, *Lapot'*, it would be better for the Straw to stretch from shore to shore. Then we could walk across on the Straw's back," replied the Bubble.

The piece of Straw stretched out from shore to shore. The *Lapot'* went first. It started walking along the Straw's back. But the Straw broke, and the *Lapot'* fell into the water.

The sight so pleased the Bubble that it began laughing. It laughed and laughed until it burst.

PART 4

TALES OF SPIRITS AND THE SUPERNATURAL

SPIRITS OF THE BATHHOUSE

Peasants used to build one-room log huts a distance from the main house for the purpose of bathing. The bathhouse contained a stove for heating water, as well as shelves and benches upon which bathers sat to wash and steam.

It was thought that evil spirits (banniki) dwelt in the bathhouse. It was considered dangerous to be alone in the bathhouse, but it was especially dangerous in the bathhouse at midnight. It was at midnight that the spirits of the bathhouse came out of hiding to play their evil tricks.

The Escape

There once was a girl who was not afraid to go to the bathhouse alone. "I'm going to the bathhouse to do my sewing," she said one day. "I'll sew a new slip for myself there, and I'll come right back home."

Taking some hot coals with her to light the darkness, she went to the bathhouse. She sat down and blew on the coals. It was midnight. She began pinning the pieces of the slip together. She looked at the pot holding the coals and saw little spirits of the bathhouse (*banniki*) blowing on the coals and jumping about all around her.

She kept sewing. Quickly, she sewed the seams of the slip together. The spirits of the bathhouse gathered around her. They hammered nails into the hem of her sarafan, which was like a pinafore.

Little by little the girl let her sarafan fall to the floor. Simultaneously, she placed the newly sewn slip over her head. Then, she jumped out of the bathhouse and ran home.

In the morning the family went to the bathhouse. There lay the girl's sarafan, ripped to shreds.

The Disappearance

One night a husband and wife went to the bathhouse. The husband washed up and wanted to go back to the house. His wife did not want to leave. She wanted to relax—to lie on the shelf and steam.

Suddenly, a spirit of the bathhouse began imitating a peacock's cry, and everyone knows that the peacock's cry is a bad omen.

The husband ran out of the bathhouse quickly. When he was outside, he remembered his wife. He ran back, but the spirit of the bathhouse, evil spirit that he was, would not let the husband back in.

The spirit of the bathhouse threw the wife's skin out the window into the man's face. "Give your wife a hug. Here's her skin for your mug," the spirit of the bathhouse shouted.

The man's wife had disappeared, and only her skin remained.

The Coffin

A fearless man once went to the bathhouse at night and did not come out for a long time. His family went to the bathhouse door to call the man, but the spirits of the bathhouse would not let the family in.

Everyone began knocking on the bathhouse door, but they only made it worse for the man.

"They are making a coffin for me," shouted the man.

The people outside could hear someone sawing and shaving wood. They heard the sound of an ax chopping.

"Now they're nailing me into the coffin," the man shouted.

The family heard the sound of nails being hammered into wood.

In the morning the family went to the bathhouse. The door was no longer locked. Inside, they found the man dead, lying in a coffin in the middle of the bathhouse.

THE WEREWOLF

There once lived an old couple. They had an only son who tried to provide for them. However hard the son worked, still they seemed to have nothing. The old people were naked, hungry, and barefoot.

One day the old man died, and the old woman sat weeping. Her son came into the cottage with a shovel.

"Why are you carrying a shovel?" the old woman asked.

"I'm going to dig a place in the garden for Father. It costs a lot of money to hire a priest, and we don't have anything. Burying him with or without a priest amounts to the same thing," said the son.

The old woman began wailing. "I'd have done better to give birth to a wolf than to give birth to such a son," she said. "What kind of son is it who wants to dig a grave for his father in the garden, as if his father were a dog?"

No sooner had she uttered these words than her son became a wolf. The wolf put his tail between his legs and ran away.

Whether he lived in the forest for a long or short time is not known, but the werewolf refused to eat uncooked meat. He would rip apart a sheep and look for the potatoes the shepherds were roasting. Then, he would cook the meat on the hot coals of the shepherd's fire. No doubt he knew that if he ate raw meat, he would remain a werewolf forever.

One winter's night he sought refuge beneath a haystack. He lay beneath the hay, shivering all over. A kind-hearted man was passing by. He caught sight of what he thought was a dog, lying there shivering, but not barking.

The man took off his long robe, called a caftan, and covered the wolf with it. As soon as the man's caftan fell onto the wolf's body, the werewolf became a man again.

The son went home and greeted his mother. His mother forgave him for his plan to bury his father in the garden. Mother and son are living happily to this very day. As to their identity, I will never tell you who they are.

THE WOOD GOBLIN GODFATHER

This story happened long ago in Tsavanga. In those days people used cradle sacks. Rather than throw out old cloth, people sewed sacks and put the children in them. Then, they could carry the children around with them wherever they went.

When haymaking time came, there was no one with whom to leave the baby, so people took their babies with them to the field. The hayfield was nearby, only about a quarter of a mile away. Nowadays there are no hayfields there. The hayfields have been cultivated and made into gardens.

They used to tie the sack with the baby in it to the branch of a tree and go to mow hay. If the baby started crying, the mother could nurse the child and return to the mowing when she was done.

One woman mowed until evening. Then, she said to her husband, "I'll go fetch the cows. They're in the forest. Don't forget to take the baby home with you."

Well, the husband kept mowing. Meanwhile, the baby was asleep. After working for a long time, until it was so dark that he could no longer see the hayfield, the husband went home. He forgot the child and left him hanging from the tree branch in the sack.

The wife came home with the cows. "Where's the baby?" she asked.

"Oh, I forgot," said the husband.

After hearing these words, the wife started running. She ran past the hill, past the swamp, and past the mown grass. She saw a stranger sitting and rocking the sack.

He was rocking the sack so hard that it swung in every direction. The woman was afraid to approach the stranger.

"If you are a man rocking the cradle, be a father to me. If you are a woman rocking the cradle, be a mother to me," she said.

The unknown person rocking the cradle said to the baby, "Your mother has left you. Your father has forgotten you."

The woman kept standing there, but the little person did not give her an answer.

"If you are a middle-aged man, be a cousin to me. If you are a middle-aged woman, be a cousin to me," the child's mother said.

The little figure kept rocking the sack, talking to the baby.

"If you are a young maiden, be a sister to me. If you are a young man, be a godfather to me," the child's mother continued.

Finally the little person spoke. "Go ahead, take the child," he said. "And I've acquired the name of godfather. Ha, ha, ha! I'm your godfather!"

The mother took her child. By then, she realized that the strange little man was a wood goblin (*leshii*), a spirit who dwells in the forest. The wood goblin likes to play tricks on people who wander into his domain. However, this little wood goblin took pity on the child and did not play any tricks on him.

From that day on the woman's cattle were never allowed to stay in the forest overnight. As soon as evening came, the little wood goblin drove the cattle home.

"Godchild's cows, go home!" he would say. Then, the cattle would head home, turning up their tails.

Whoever was mowing at the time would hear him say, "Godchild's cow, go home!'

This happened in the countryside, in the village of Tsavanga. My mother had some fields there, and that is how I know about it.

In the old days, of course, they believed that the wood goblin led people astray in the forest and caused them to get lost. Nowadays people do not believe anything of the sort. And the wood goblins don't lead people astray anymore.

THE HOUSE SPIRIT

The house spirit (domovoi) *protects the home, looking after the livestock and guarding the hearth. He lives in a nook behind the stove.*

Father was telling a story about how to get a glimpse of a house spirit. Of course, the house spirit does not like to be seen. "If you want to see a house spirit," said father, "take a clean comb and pour out a bucket of water. Make certain that the water is clean. Throw the comb into the water. Three days later there will be a house spirit's hair in it.

"One time we did just that," continued Father. "After three days had passed, we looked in the bucket. Sure enough, a hair was there, a gray-white hair.

"If you rub this hair in your hands, the light will be extinguished. It will go out, so to speak. If you rub the hair, the house spirit will appear."

When I got home, I followed Father's instruction. I poured some clean water into a bucket and threw a comb into it. Sure enough, three days later a house spirit's hair was in the water. I rubbed the hair, but nothing happened.

The next day I rubbed the hair at night and saw an old man. He was kind of white. He was naked with white and gray hair that was all overgrown. He had a long beard. In short, he was a little old man.

I sat down at once and was so scared that I couldn't utter a single word. The house spirit sat there for a while, and then—well, I never—I looked and he wasn't there. Just like that, he wasn't there.

Later, in the morning, I told Father about it. "Well, it's lucky you saw him," Father said. "It means that you'll live a happy life."

THE BRIDE FROM THE HAUNTED HOUSE

This story happened long ago when there were frights and mysteries. Of course, nowadays there are no frights or mysteries anymore.

A man had an only son. When the son grew up, he would take walks in the village on pleasant evenings. One of the houses he passed was empty. He passed it many times and never heard any noise coming from it.

One day as he was passing the abandoned house, he heard someone crying, "Come here! Your bride awaits you."

He returned home immediately and said not a word to his parents.

"Why did you come home so early today?" they asked.

The young man was silent. The next evening, as he was passing the abandoned house, once again he heard a voice crying, "Come here! Your bride awaits you."

He returned home and lay on his bed. He kept silent and said not a word to anyone.

The third evening he went to the house, he heard the cry again. "Come today and take away your bride. If you don't, you'll be sorry."

The young man rushed home and finally broke his silence. "Mama and Papa," he said, "someone in the abandoned house has been crying for the third evening in a row. They cry, 'Come here! Your bride is waiting. Take her away, or you'll be sorry.' "

His mother and father ran to get the boy's godfather. They took a holy icon with them and went to the haunted house.

They entered the house and saw three maidens sitting inside. One girl winked at them. The young man took her wink to mean that she was his intended bride. He pointed at her to indicate that she was his. The godfather held the icon over her head. She remained, and the other two maidens disappeared.

The girl said that an evil spirit had brought her there from a foreign land. He had brought many young women to the house, where they made so much trouble for the spirit that he began giving them away. The bride was very happy indeed to have escaped him.

The couple went straight from the haunted house to the church to be married. From that day on they lived together in happiness.

ACTIVITIES TO ACCOMPANY THE STORIES

After reading these tales, try your hand at some Russian folk crafts, recipes, riddles, and other activities linked to specific tales. There are not activities for all stories, but those selected are listed in the order they appear in the Contents.

Kolobok, the Runaway Bun

Follow the recipe below, and make some runaway buns of your own.

Runaway Buns

Ingredients

1 egg

⅓ cup sugar

⅓ cup sour cream

1 cup flour

½ teaspoon baking soda

¾ teaspoon baking powder

¼ teaspoon salt

vegetable oil, for frying

powdered or maple sugar

Directions

Beat the egg, then add sugar; mix well. Stir in sour cream. Sift flour, baking soda, baking powder, and salt together. Add dry ingredients to the egg and sour cream mixture. Place the dough in the refrigerator to chill.

Knead small pieces of dough on a floured board. Shape the dough into small, round buns. Let the buns sit drying for 15 minutes.

Cook on both sides in hot oil, then place on a paper towel to absorb the oil. Dust with powdered sugar or maple sugar. Makes 12–14 small, round buns.

Warning: Do not place the runaway buns on the windowsill, or they may roll away!

Tails

Decorative hand-drawn or engraved folk prints were known as *lubki* (plural form). They resemble comic books because more space is devoted to pictures than to text. The *lubok* (singular form) was a bright, simply drawn sheet or chapbook that was sold at a reasonable price. Consequently, it was available to the common folk. Typical themes of the *lubki* were folktales and fairy tales, novels, songs, satires, history, and geography. Religious *lubki* originated in the latter half of the seventeenth century, and secular *lubki* appeared at the beginning of the eighteenth century. By the end of the nineteenth century, *lubki* were no longer created.

Initially, *lubki* were hand-drawn or carved by anonymous artists on wooden printing blocks, from which prints were made. Later, pictures and texts were engraved on copper plates. Finally, *lubki* were created using a more modern lithographic process in which sheets were printed from flat stones.

Create your own *lubok,* or chapbook, by drawing a print representing each animal in the story "Tails" and the tail it chose. Draw the fox with her fluffy tail, the horse with his long tail, and the cow with her broom tail. Include pictures of the pig, the elephant, the bear, the wolf, and the rabbit. Use bright watercolors, magic markers, or crayons to color the animals.

Next write a caption under each of your pictures. For example, under the picture of the fox, you might write, "See what a magnificent tail I selected for myself!" When your book is completed, you will have learned about an old Russian folk art—the *lubok.*

The Winged, Hairy, and Buttery Friends

Bliny are an ancient Slavic dish. In pagan days, the ancient Slavs made round *bliny* that looked like the sun, which they worshipped. Today Russians prepare *bliny* for wakes or funeral feasts and for the Shrovetide carnival called *maslenitsa.*

In the story entitled "The Winged, Hairy, and Buttery Friends," a sparrow, a mouse, and a buttery pancake (called a *blin*) are friends. Follow the recipe below to make *bliny* (plural form). Once you have made your *bliny*, keep them at home; do not let them go to the forest, or Patrikeevna the Fox may gobble them up.

Note: *Bliny* are traditionally made with buckwheat flour, but this lighter, more modern version will appeal to anyone who enjoys pancakes.

Russian Pancakes (bliny)

Ingredients

2–3 eggs

3 cups warm water

½ teaspoon salt

1 tablespoon sugar

½ teaspoon baking soda

3¾ cups flour

½ teaspoon lemon juice

1 cup water

vegetable oil, for frying

butter, sour cream, and jam for topping

Directions

Beat eggs into 3 cups of warm water. Add salt, sugar, and baking soda. Then, beat the flour into the mixture until there are no lumps in the dough. Mix the lemon juice into a cup of water. Pour it into the dough mixture and beat. Fry the pancakes (*bliny*) in a frying pan to which vegetable oil has been added. Keep the bottom of the pan covered with vegetable oil.

Serve the pancakes with butter, sour cream, and jam to be spread on top.

The Snow Maiden

Create a Snow Maiden out of snow.

Materials

Red food coloring, kerchief, large buttons for eyes and nose, red yarn for mouth, shawl for shoulders.

Directions

Make a snowball and roll it in the snow until a large ball has formed. Make a medium-sized ball in the same manner and place it on top of the large ball. Now make a small ball and place it on top of the medium ball; it will be the Snow Maiden's head.

Now decorate your Snow Maiden. Create button eyes and a button nose. Make a mouth with the red yarn and curve it into a smile; place it on the Snow Maiden's face. Color the cheeks with the red food coloring. Tie a kerchief around the Snow Maiden's head and tie a shawl around the middle ball, which forms her shoulders.

Remember that should your Snow Maiden melt, you can repeat the process next year, and the Snow Maiden will come back to you.

Father Frost

Russians erect and decorate fir trees in their homes as part of the New Year's celebration. At home and at school, during the New Year's children's party (*utrennik*), children hold hands and dance around the tree while singing.

Make decorations for the fir tree beneath which the heroine of "Father Frost" sat after her mean stepmother sent her off into the forest.

Equipment

Pencil, scissors, compass or jar cover (approximately 3 inches in diameter), and needle.

Materials

Multicolored construction paper, glue, thread, sequins, beads, trim, candies, and nuts.

Directions

Using the compass or jar cover, trace and cut out 3 circles, each approximately 3 inches in diameter, from construction paper.

Basket ornament: Cut a slit to the center of the circle and form the paper into a pyramid basket. Glue the cut ends together. Cut a strip of construction paper 4 inches long and ½ inch wide. Glue it to the basket to serve as a handle. Put candies or nuts into the basket.

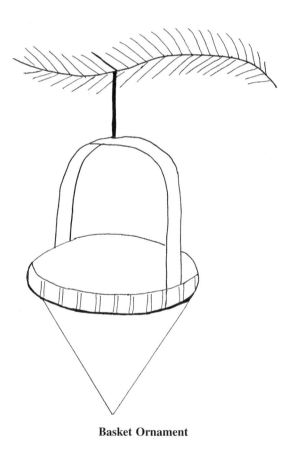

Basket Ornament

Pyramid ornament: Place two pyramids constructed as described above together so that they are joined at the wide ends. Sew the pyramids together with thread at the wide ends.

Decorate the basket and the joined pyramids with beads, sequins, and trim. Fasten a thread around the handle of the basket and loop a thread through the top of the joined pyramids so that you can hang your ornaments on the tree.

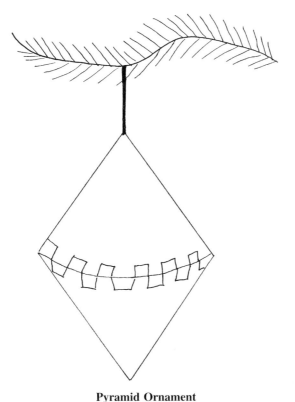

Pyramid Ornament

The Puff Monster

Make a puff monster out of polyester fiberfill.

Equipment

Hot glue gun and scissors.

Materials

Glue sticks, polyester fiberfill, beads, sequins (stars and moons), glitter, pieces of black and red yarn, and animal eyes or buttons.

Directions

Shape a large clump of polyester fiberfill into a large round ball. Use the hot glue gun to glue on animal eyes, red yarn mouth, black yarn nose, and black yarn wrinkles

---

onto the puff monster's face. Create as fierce an expression as possible. Now use the beads and sequins to decorate your monster. Glue sequin stars and moons onto your monster, or sprinkle glitter onto him.

The Enchanted Princess

In the nineteenth century Russian peasant women wore long shirts covered with a sarafan, a long jumper. Men, too, wore a tunic-like shirt over their pants. In addition, the peasants used towels, tablecloths, and bed linen, all white in color. To make the white cloth more colorful, women embroidered it with cheerful motifs.

Draw and embroider the magic tree described in "The Enchanted Princess." To try your hand at Russian embroidery, you will need the items listed below.

Equipment

Embroidery needle, embroidery hoop (optional), scissors, and pencil.

Material

Paper, piece of white cloth 12 inches in length and width, varied colors of embroidery thread, beads, and sequins.

Directions

Draw the tree on paper. Cut out the drawing and trace with a pencil onto a 12 by 12 inch square of white cloth. Or, if you are a good artist, try drawing the tree in pencil right onto the cloth. Now draw apples, pears, and singing birds in the tree branches.

You will need to know two embroidery stitches, the stem stitch and the satin stitch. The stem stitch is used wherever you have drawn a line. Wherever you want to add body and fill in with color, use the satin stitch. For example, you may want to use the stem stitch in dark green to outline the leaves on the tree and the satin stitch in light green to fill in the leaves with color.

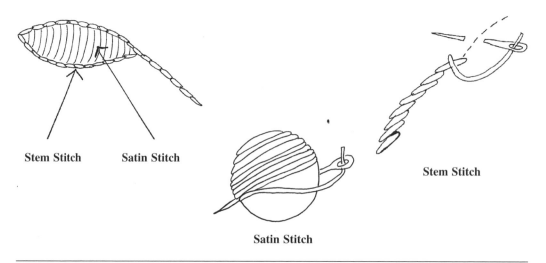

Stem Stitch   Satin Stitch

Satin Stitch

Stem Stitch

Activities to Accompany the Stories

The Egg

Russian folk artists paint fairytale scenes, churches, geometric designs, flowers, animals, and similar motifs onto wooden eggs, which are lacquered afterward. Create your own magic egg. Experiment with designing a peasant doll on a wooden egg. These can be purchased at most craft stores.

Equipment

Hot glue gun, pen, and magic markers.

Materials

Wooden eggs, glue sticks, beads, sequins, and fancy ribbon trim.

Directions

Holding the egg on one side, draw a round circle (the face) with a pen or thin-tipped magic marker on the upper (narrow) end of the side facing you. Draw smaller circles around the round circle (the headdress). Draw a vertical line down the middle of the egg from the doll's neck to the bottom of the egg (wide end). Glue, the fancy ribbon trim onto this line. Draw eyes, a nose, and a mouth on the face with pen or thin-tipped markers. Now decorate the doll's headdress and sarafan with beads and sequins. The back of the egg, which is the back of the doll's sarafan, can be decorated, too.

The Egg

A Copeck a Drop

Prepare cabbage soup (*shchi*) for the soldier in the story. Unlike the old woman, you may be generous with the oil and pour as many drops as you like into the soup.

Cabbage Soup (Shchi)

Ingredients

2 chicken legs

2 diced potatoes

1 shredded cabbage

1 grated carrot

1 diced tomato

1 diced onion

salt to taste

clove of garlic

sprig of dill and parsley

olive oil

Directions

Boil the chicken legs gently in salted water until the meat falls off the bone. Separate the meat from the bone and throw it back into the stockpot. Discard skin and bones. Throw in the diced potatoes, and let them boil. Sauté the cabbage, carrot, tomato, and onion in olive oil. Add the mixture to the stockpot. Salt to taste. Add a clove of garlic and dill and parsley to taste. When the potato is cooked through and tender, the soup is ready to eat. Don't forget to add several drops of olive oil. A dollop of sour cream may also be added to the soup before eating it.

The Sorcerer

Beetle, the sorcerer, was apt at solving riddles, although his solutions were mainly a matter of good luck rather than clairvoyance. Do you know the answers to the Russian riddles below? Riddles are translated from V. P. Anikin's collection entitled *Chernyi kon' skachet v ogon',* Shkol'naia biblioteka (Moscow: Detskaia literatura, 1968).

1. What has no hands and no feet, but can tap-tap at the windowpane begging to be let in?
2. What sits on a spoon and dangles its legs?
3. What has two bellies and four ears?
4. What flies about in a white coat that has no buttons?
5. I sit on a tree. I am round as a ball, red as blood, and sweet as honey. What am I?
6. What is tied tight, yet dances around the room?
7. Fire cannot burn it. Water cannot drown it. What is it?
8. What has teeth but does not bite?
9. What spreads a net but does not catch fish?
10. What wears several dresses at the same time and still feels the cold?

Answers: 1. Wind 2. Noodles 3. Pillow 4. Snow 5. Cherry 6. Broom 7. Ice 8. Rake 9. Spider 10. Cabbage. (A cabbage has several layers of leaves and feels cold.)

The Fool and the Birch Tree

Russians have a special love of the birch tree. They compare the birch to a beautiful maiden letting down her hair. Birch bark weaving is a traditional folk craft. It developed in northern Russia. Baskets, round boxes, headbands, bast shoes (*lapti*), and water flasks are made from birch bark. Designs are carved on the bark. It is said that anything stored in a birch bark container, such as grain or water, takes on the healing properties of the tree and is good for one's health. Useful even in its demise, the dead birch of the story entitled "The Fool and the Birch Tree" held a treasure in its hollow.

Equipment

Stapler or sewing needle, scissors.

Materials

Thread, birch bark, or reeds used in basket weaving.

Directions

Try your hand at making a headband of birch bark or reeds. First, cut the bark into narrow strips long enough to encircle your head one and a half times, or use a reed of equal length. Then, soak the strips in water until they are soft and pliable. Staple, or sew, the ends of three birch strips together, and braid them while they are damp. If you cannot find birch bark, use bark or wooden strips used in basket weaving. Size the braid to your head. Cut off any excess. Staple or sew the ends of completed braid so that the braid is circular. Then, wear your birch bark headband. Perhaps it will bring you health and happiness.

BIBLIOGRAPHY

Afanas'ev, A. N., comp. *Narodnye russkie skazki*. 8 vols. 1855–1863. Reprint (6th ed., 3 vols.) with an introduction by V. Ia. Propp, Moscow: Gosudarstvennoe Izdatel'stvo Khudozhestvennoi Literatury, 1957.

———. *Narodnye russkie skazki*. 3 vols. Moscow: Goslitizdat, 1958. Reprint (selections), Moscow: Khudozhestvennaia literatura, 1977.

———. *Narodnye russkie skazki*. 3 vols. Moscow: Goslitizdat, 1958. Reprint (2 vols.), Moscow: Sovetskaia Rossiia, 1978–1981.

———. *Russkie detskie skazki*. Ed. È. V. Pomerantseva. Moscow: Detskaia literatura, 1961.

Akimov, T. M., comp. *Fol'klor Saratovskoi oblasti*. Saratov, Russia: Saratovskoe oblastnoe izdatel'stvo, 1946.

Anikin, V. P., comp. *Detstvo. Otrochestvo: Skazki o zhivotnykh, volshebnye, bytovye, balagurnye, dokuchnye, nebylitsty, zagadki*. Vol. 2. Mudrost' narodnaia, zhizn' cheloveka v russkom fol'klore, eds. V. P. Anikin, V. E. Gusev, and N. I. Tolstoi. Moscow: Khudozhestvennaia literatura, 1994.

———. *Russkie narodnye skazki*. Moscow: Detskaia literatura, 1976.

———. *Zhivaia voda, sbornik russkikh narodnykh pesen, skazok, poslovits, zagadok*. Moscow: Detskaia literatura, 1975.

Azadovskii, M. K., ed. *Skazki Filippa Pavlovicha Gospodareva*. Recorded by N. V. Novikov. Nauchno-issledovatel'skii Institut kul'tury K-FSSR. Petrozavodsk: Gosizdat K-FSSR, 1941.

Balashov, D. M., comp. *Skazki Terskogo berega Belogo moria*. Ed. È. V. Pomerantseva. Academiia nauk SSSR: Karel'skii filial, Institut iazyka, literatury i istorii. Leningrad: Nauka, 1970.

Bazanov, V. G., and O. B. Alekseeva, eds. *Velikorusskie skazki v zapisiakh I. A. Khudiakova*. Moscow and Leningrad: Nauka, 1964.

Bogoliubskaia, M. K., and A. L. Tabenkina, comps. *Khrestomatiia po detskoi literature; Uchebnoe posobie dlia doshkol'nykh pedagogicheskikh uchilishch*. 5th ed. Moscow: Prosveshchenie, 1968.

————. *Nashi skazki, russkie narodnye skazki, pesenki, zagadki.* Vol. 1. Bibliotechka det-skogo sada. Moscow: Detskaia literatura, 1965.

Bulatov, M., retold by. *Morozko.* Moscow: Malysh, 1989.

————. *Teremok.* 2nd ed. Moscow: Malysh, 1969.

Chernyshev, V. I., recorded by. *Skazki i legendy Pushkinskikh mest.* Moscow and Leningrad: Izdatel'stvo Akademii nauk SSSR, 1950.

Galkin, P., M. Kitainik, and N. Kushtum, comps. and eds. *Russkie narodnye skazki Urala.* Sverdlovsk, Russia: Sverdlovskoe knizhnoe izdatel'stvo, 1959.

Gavrilovich, V. G., L. F. Klimanova, L. K. Piskunova, and L. S. Gellershtein, comps. *Kniga dlia chteniia: Uchebnik dlia 2 klassa trekhletnei nachal'noi shkoly v dvukh chasti-akh.* 4th ed. 2 vols. Moscow: Prosveshchenie, 1989.

————. *Rodnoe slovo: Uchebnik po chteniiu dlia uchashchikhsia 2 klassa chetyrekh let-nei nachal'noi shkoly.* 3rd ed. Moscow: Prosveshchenie, 1989.

Gofman, È., and S. Mints, recorded by. *Skazki I. F. Kovalev.* Ed. Iu. M. Sokolov. Moscow: Gosudarstvennyi literaturnyi muzei, 1941.

Karnaukhova, I., retold by. *Nenagliadnaia krasota: Russkie volshebnye skazki.* 3rd ed. Moscow: Detskaia literatura, 1973.

Karpinskaia, N., and P. Dymshits, comps. *Tvoia kniga: Sbornik dlia chteniia v sem'e i v detskom sadu.* Bibliotechka detskogo sada. Moscow: Detskaia literatura, 1968.

Komovskaia, N. D. *Predaniia i skazki Gor'kovskoi oblasti.* Gorkii, Russia: n. p., 1951.

Kovacheva, N. N., and A. V. Frolkina, comps. *Russkie skazki (Russian Fairy-Tales), a Rus-sian Reader with Explanatory Notes in English.* Introductory article by A. V. Kulagina. Moscow: Russkii iazyk, 1984.

Kravtsov, N. I., and A. V. Kulagina, comps. *Slavianskii fol'klor.* Moscow: Izdatel'stvo Moskovskogo universiteta, 1987.

Kulagina, A. V., comp. *Russkoe ustnoe narodnoe tvorchestvo: Khrestomatiia.* Moscow: Iz-datel'stvo Rossiiskoi akademii obrazovaniia, 1996.

Kulagina, A. V., and Bonnie C. Marshall, comp. and trans. "Russian Folklore: A Bilingual Text." In production, Moscow State University Press.

Pomerantseva, È. V., ed. *Skazki Abrama Novopol'tseva.* Kuibyshev: Kuibyshevskoe oblast-noe gosudarstvennoe izdatel'stvo, 1952.

Russkie skazki pro zverei. Kemerovo, Russia: Kemerovskoe knizhnoe izdatel'stvo, 1961.

Selivanov, F. M., comp. *Khrestomatiia po fol'kloru: Kniga dlia shkol'nikov.* Moscow: Prosveshchenie, 1972.

Shastina, Elena, comp. *Skazki Lenskikh beregov.* Irkutsk, Russia: Vostochno-sibirskoe knizhnoe izdatel'stvo, 1971.

Tolstoi, A. N., retold by. *Kolobok.* Moscow: Detskaia literatura, 1969.

————. *Russkie narodnye skazki v obrabotke A. N. Tolstogo.* Moscow: Detskaia literatura, 1965.

Vorob"eva, I., comp. *Koleso: Russkie narodnye satiricheskie i zabavnye skazki.* 2nd ed. Shkol'naia biblioteka. Moscow: Detskaia literatura, 1967.

—————, ed. *Russkie volshebnye skazki.* Moscow: Detskaia literatura, 1970.

Zelenin, D. K. *Velikorusskie skazki Permskoi gubernii.* 1914. Reprint, Moscow: Pravda, 1991.

RECOMMENDED READINGS IN ENGLISH

History and Geography

Acton, Edward. *Russia: The Tsarist and Soviet Legacy*. 2nd ed. Present and Past Series. White Plains, NY: Longman, 1995.

Corona, Laurel. *The Russian Federation*. Modern Nations of the World Series. San Diego: Lucent Books, 2001.

Edwards, Mike. "A Broken Empire, After the Soviet Union's Collapse: Russia, Kazakhstan, Ukraine." *National Geographic* 183, no. 2 (August 1994): 100–115.

Fitzpatrick, Sheila. *Everyday Stalinism: Ordinary Life in Extraordinary Times. Soviet Russia in the 1930s*. Oxford, England: Oxford University Press, 2000.

Gilbert, Martin. *Routledge Atlas of Russian History: From 800 BC to the Present Day*. 2nd ed. London: Routledge, 1995.

Gorbachev, Mikhail. *On My Country and the World*. Trans. George Shriver. Boulder: University Press of Colorado, 1999.

Graves, William, ed. *Communism to Capitalism*. Cartographer John F. Shupe. Map supplement to *National Geographic* 183, no. 3 (March 1993).

Greenall, Robert. "The People's Will." *Russian Life* 39, no. 6 (June 1996): 4–9.

Likhachev, Dmitry, ed. *A History of Russian Literature: 11th–17th Centuries*. Trans. K. M. Cook-Horujy. Moscow: Raduga Publishers, 1989.

Massimo, Salvadori. *The Rise of Modern Communism: A Brief History of the Communist Movement in the Twentieth Century*. Berkshire Studies in Russian History. New York: Henry Holt, 1952.

Pavlenko, Nikolai Ivanovich. "A Woman of Substance." *Russian Life* 39, no. 11 (November 1996): 4–10.

Raeff, Marc. *Origins of the Russian Intelligentsia: The Eighteenth-Century Nobility*. New York: Harcourt, Brace and World, 1966.

Service, Robert W. *A History of Twentieth-Century Russia*. Cambridge, MA: Harvard University Press, 1999.

Shipler, David. *Russia: Broken Idols, Solemn Dreams*. New York: Times Books, 1983, 1989; Harmondsworth, England: Penguin, 1989.

Vucinich, Wayne S., ed. *The Peasant in Nineteenth-Century Russia*. Stanford, CA: Stanford University Press, 1968.

Yurganov, Andrei. "The Father of Tsarism." *Russian Life* 40, no. 1 (January 1997): 12–18.

Folklore, Mythology, and Culture

Adelman, Deborah. *The "Children of Perestroika" Come of Age: Young People of Moscow Talk about Life in the New Russia*. Armonk, NY: M. E. Sharpe, 1994.

Alexinsky, G. "Slavonic Mythology." *New Larousse Encyclopedia of Mythology*. New York: Prometheus Press, 1959. 293–310.

Barker, Adele M. *Consuming Russia: Popular Culture, Sex and Society since Gorbachev*. Durham, NC: Duke University Press, 1999.

———. *The Mother Syndrome in the Russian Folk Imagination*. Columbus, OH: Slavica, 1986.

Bickman, Connie. *Children of Russia*. Through the Eyes of Children Series. Edina, MN: ABDO Publishing Company, 1994.

Billington, James H. *The Icon and the Axe: An Interpretive History of Russian Culture*. New York: Vintage Books, 1970.

Boym, Svetlana. *Common Places: Mythologies of Everyday Life in Russia*. Cambridge, MA: Harvard University Press, 1996.

Burckhardt, Ann L. *The People of Russia and Their Food*. Multicultural Cookbooks Series. Mankato, MN: Capstone Press, 1996.

Gimbutas, Marija. "Ancient Slavic Religion: A Synopsis." *To Honor Roman Jakobson. Essays on the Occasion of His Seventieth Birthday, 11 October 1966*. The Hague: Mouton, 1967. 1: 738–759.

Gorer, Geoffrey, et al. *Russian Culture*. Study of Contemporary Western Culture, vol. 3. Herndon, VA: Berghahn Books, 2001.

Hubbs, Joanna. *Mother Russia: The Feminine Myth in Russian Culture*. Bloomington: Indiana University Press, 1988.

Ivanits, Linda J. *Russian Folk Belief*. 1989. Reprint, Armonk, NY: M. E. Sharpe, 1992.

Jakobson, Roman. "Slavic Mythology." *Funk and Wagnalls Standard Dictionary of Folklore, Mythology, and Legend*. 2 vols. New York: Crowell, 1950. 1025–1028.

Likhachev, Dmitry S. *Reflections on the Russian Soul: A Memoir*. New York: Central European University Press, 2000.

Mann, Robert. *Russian Apocalypse: Songs and Tales about the Coming of Christianity to Russia*. Lawrence, KS: Coronado Press, 1986.

Maranda, Pierre, ed. *Soviet Structural Folkloristics*. Approaches to Semiotics, no. 42. The Hague: Mouton, 1974.

Miller, Frank J. *Folklore for Stalin: Russian Folklore and Pseudofolklore of the Stalin Era*. Studies of the Harriman Institute. Armonk, NY: M.E. Sharpe, 1990.

Nemirovskaya, Julia. *Inside the Russian Soul: An Historical Survey of Russian Cultural Patterns*. Berkeley, CA: McGraw-Hill/Osborne, 1997.

Oinas, Felix J. *Essays on Russian Folklore and Mythology*. 1984. Reprint, Columbus, OH: Slavica, 1985.

Oinas, Felix J., and Stephen Soudakoff, eds. *The Study of Russian Folklore*. Indiana University Folklore Institute Monograph Series, vol. 25. The Hague and Paris: Mouton, 1975.

Pirkova-Jakobson, Svatava. "Slavic Folklore." *Funk and Wagnalls Standard Dictionary of Folklore, Mythology, and Legend*. 2 vols. New York: Crowell, 1950. 1019–1025.

Propp, Vladimir. *Theory and History of Folklore*. Ed. with an introduction and notes by Anatoly Liberman. Trans. Ariadna Y. Martin, Richard P. Martin, et al. Theory and History of Literature 5. Minneapolis: University of Minnesota Press, 1984.

Ralphs, E. E., comp and trans. *A Bear Book: The Bear in Russian Literature and Folklore*. Edinburgh, Scotland: Charles Skilton, 1985.

———. *The Cat in Russian Literature and Folklore*. Edinburgh, Scotland: Charles Skilton, 1984.

Ryan, W. F. *The Bathhouse at Midnight: An Historical Survey of Magic and Divination in Russia*. Magic in History Series. University Park: Pennsylvania State University Press, 1999.

Toomre, Joyce, and Musya Glants, eds. *Food in Russian History and Culture*. Indiana-Michigan Series in Russian and East European Studies. Bloomington: Indiana University Press, 1997.

Studies of the Folktale

Carey, Bonnie Marshall. "Typological Models of the Heroine in the Russian Fairy Tale." Diss. (Ph.D.). The University of North Carolina at Chapel Hill, 1983.

Gilet, Peter. *Vladimir Propp and the Universal Folktale: Recommissioning an Old Paradigm—Story as Initiation*. Middlebury Studies in Russian Language and Literature, vol. 17. Bern, Berlin, Bruxelles, Frankfurt, New York: Peter Lang, 1998.

Harkins, William E. "Folk Tales." *Dictionary of Russian Literature*. 1956. Reprint, Westport, CT: Greenwood, 1976. 122–124.

Jakobson, Roman. "Commentaries on Russian Fairy Tales." *Selected Writings*. Vol. 4. 1975. Reprint, The Hague and Paris: Mouton, 1966. 82–101.

Kravchenko, Maria. *The World of the Russian Fairy Tale*. Berne and New York: Peter Lang, 1987.

Propp, Vladimir Ia. *Morphology of the Folktale*. Trans. Lawrence Scott. Intro Alan Dundes. Publications of the American Folklore Society. Bibliographical and Special Series, vol. 9. 1958. Reprint, Austin: University of Texas, 1968.

———. "Transformations in Fairy Tales." *Mythology: Selected Readings*. Ed. Pierre Maranda. Middlesex, England: Penguin Books, 1972. 139–150.

Wosien, Maria-Gabriele. *The Russian Folk-Tale: Some Structural and Thematic Aspects*. Slavistische Beitrage, no. 41. Munich: Sagner, 1969.

Yovino-Young, Marjorie. *Pagan Ritual and Myth in Russian Magic Tales: A Study of Patterns*. Lewiston, NY: E. Mellen Press, 1993.

Folktale Collections

Afanas'ev, A. N. *Russian Fairy Tales*. Trans. Norbert Guterman. Commentary by Roman Jakobson. 3rd ed. New York: Pantheon Books, 1976.

———. *Russian Folk Tales*. Trans. Natalie Duddington. 1967. Reprint, New York: Funk and Wagnalls, 1969.

———. *Russian Folk-Tales*. Intro and notes by Leonard A. Magnus. London: Kegan Paul, Trench, Trubner, 1916; New York: E.P. Dutton, 1916; Ann Arbor, MI: Gryphon Books, 1971; Detroit: Gale Research Co., 1974.

———. *Russian Folk Tales*. Trans. Robert Chandler. New York: Random House, 1980.

Almedingen, Edith Martha. *Russian Folk and Fairy Tales*. 1957. Reprint, New York: Putnam, 1963.

Avery, Gillian, and Arthur Ransome. *Russian Fairy Tales*. Everyman's Library Children's Classics Series. New York: Alfred A. Knopf, 1995.

Budberg, Moura, trans. and comp. *Russian Fairy Tales*. 1965. Reprint, New York: F. Warne, 1967.

Carey, Bonnie Marshall, trans. and comp. *Baba Yaga's Geese and Other Russian Stories*. Bloomington: Indiana University Press, 1973.

Carpenter, Frances. *Tales of a Russian Grandmother*. 1933. Reprint, Garden City, NY: Doubleday, Doran and Co., 1935.

Cook, Kathleen, James Riordan, Olga Shartse, et al., trans. *On Seashore Far a Green Oak Towers: A Book of Tales*. Moscow: Raduga Publishers, 1983.

Curtin, Jeremiah. *Myths and Folk-Tales of the Russians, Western Slavs, and the Magyars*. London: Sampson, Low, Marston, 1890; Boston: Little, Brown, and Co., 1903, 1971, 1977. Reprint, New York: Benjamin Blom, 1990.

Daniels, Guy, trans. *The Falcon under the Hat: Russian Merry Tales and Fairy Tales*. New York: Funk and Wagnalls, 1969.

Dietrich, Anton, comp. *Russian Popular Tales*. Intro. by Jacob Grimm. 1857. Reprint, Norwood, PA: Norwood Editions, 1974.

Dolch, Edward W., and Marguerite P. Dolch, eds. *Stories from Old Russia*. Folklore of the World. Champaign, IL: Garrard, 1964.

Downing, Charles, retold by. *Russian Tales and Legends*. London: Oxford University Press, 1956.

Gerber, Adolph. *Great Russian Animal Tales. A Collection of Fifty Tales, with an Introduction, a Synopsis of the Adventures and Motives, a Discussion of the Same and Appendix*. Burt Franklin Research and Source Works, no. 630. Essays in Literature and Criticism 107. 1891. Reprint, New York: B. Franklin, 1970.

Gissing, Vera, trans. *Russian Fairy Tales*. World Fairy Tales Series. London: Hamlyn, 1975.

Haney, Jack V. *Russian Animal Tales*. The Complete Russian Folktale, vol. 2. Armonk, NY: M.E. Sharpe, 1999.

———. *Russian Wondertales I: Tales of Heroes and Villains*. The Complete Russian Folktale, vol. 3. Armonk, NY: M.E. Sharpe, 2001.

———. *Russian Wondertales II: Tales of Magic and the Supernatural*. The Complete Russian Folktale, vol. 4. Armonk, NY: M.E. Sharpe, 2001.

Haviland, Virginia. *Favorite Fairy Tales Told in Russia*. Retold from Russian Storytellers. New York: Morrow Beechtree Paperback Book, 1961.

Isaacs, Bernard, and Irina Zheleznova, trans. *The Fire Bird: Russian Fairy Tales*. 1900. Reprint, Moscow: Progress Publishers, 1979.

Lord, Albert Bates, ed. *Russian Folk Tales*. New York: Members of the Limited Editions Club, 1970.

MacKenzie, Donald. *Folk Tales from Russia*. Library of Folklore. New York: Hippocrene Books, 1999.

Maxym, Lucy. *Russian Lacquer, Legends and Fairy Tales*. 1981, 1982, 1984, 1985. Reprint, Manhasset, NY: Siamese Imports Co., 1987.

Onassis, Jacqueline, ed. *The Firebird and Other Russian Fairy Tales*. New York: Viking Press, 1978.

Polevoi, Peter Nikolaevich. *Russian Fairy Tales from the Skazki of Polevoi*. Trans. R. Nisbet Bain. London: Lawrence and Bullen, 1892, 1893; Chicago: Way and Williams, 1895; London: A. H. Bullen, 1901; London: G.G. Harrap and Co., 1915.

Ponsot, Marie, trans. *Russian Fairy Tales*. New York: Golden Press, 1960.

Ralston, William Ralston Shedden. *Russian Fairy Tales: A Choice Collection of Muscovite Folklore*. 1880. Reprint, New York: Hurst, 1889.

———. *Russian Folk-Tales*. International Folklore Series. London: Smith Elder and Co., 1873. New York: Arno Press, 1977.

Ransome, Arthur. *Old Peter's Russian Tales*. London: T.C. and E.C. Jack, 1925; New York: T. Nelson, 1935, 1938; New York: Dover, 1969; London: Nelson, 1971; Harmondsworth, England: Puffin Books, 1974.

Steele, Robert, ed. *The Russian Garland of Fairy Tales: Being Russian Folk Legends. Translated from a Collection of Chapbooks Made in Moscow.* New York: Kraus Reprint Co., 1971.

Warner, Elizabeth. *Heroes, Monsters, and Other Worlds from Russian Mythology.* World Mythologies Series. New York: Schocken Books, 1985.

Wheeler, Post. *Russian Wonder Tales.* New York: The Century Co., 1912; London: A. and C. Black, 1917; New York: The Century Co., 1919; New York: The Beechhurst Press, 1946 (revised); New York: Thomas Yoseloff, 1957.

White, Anne Terry, comp. *Czar of the Water. The Humpbacked Horse.* Champaign, IL: Garrard Publishing Co., 1968.

Xenophontovna, Verra, et al., retold by. *Folk Tales from the Russian.* Great Neck, NY: Core Collection Books, 1979.

Zheleznova, Irina L'vovna, ed. *Vasilisa the Beautiful: Russian Fairy Tales.* Progress Publishers, 1966.

INDEX

Volshebnye skazki. See Fairy tales
"Vulgar sociologism," 17

War Communism, 8
Water of life, 73
Werewolf, 20. *See also* "The Werewolf"
"The Werewolf," 119
West Slavs, 5
Whiner the Mosquito. *See* "The Mansion-House"
Whites, 8
"The Winged, Hairy, and Buttery Friends," 47–49
Winter Palace, 7
Witch. *See* Baba Yaga; "Magic Water"
Wolf, 19, 126
    "Cheeky the Goat, 52–55
    "*Kolobok*, the Runaway Bun," 27–29
    "The Mansion-House," 30–32
    "Tails," 33–34
    "Vaska the Cat," 37–39
    "The Werewolf," 119

"The Wolf and the Old Man's Daughters," 40–42
"The Wolf and the Old Man's Daughters," 19, 40–42
Wood goblin (*leshii*), 20. *See also* "The Wood Goblin Godfather"
"The Wood Goblin Godfather," 120–121
World War I, 1, 7
World War II, 8–9

Yanev, Gennadii (Vice President), 10
Yeltsin, Boris, 10 *See* Unnumbered photo section
Yenisei, 1. *See also* Physical Map of Russia
Yoke, 95, 96

Zakuski, 12, 86
Zavalinka, 49
Zavarka (tea brew). *See* Unnumbered photo section
Zelenin, D. K., 15

About the Author

BONNIE C. MARSHALL, author, teacher, translator, and folklorist, is Adjunct Associate Professor of Russian and Curriculum Coordinator of the Russian Program at Johnson C. Smith University. A native of New Hampshire, she received her education from Boston University, Assumption College, and The University of North Carolina, as well as from three institutions of higher learning in Russia (Moscow State University, Leningrad State University, and the Herzen Institute). Dr. Marshall has taught at Davidson College, the University of South Alabama, the University of Montana, the College of the Holy Cross, and at other universities in the United States, as well as at The School for Global Education and the American Academy of Foreign Languages in Russia. Her collection of Russian folklore entitled *Baba Yaga's Geese and Other Russian Stories* won the Chicago Book Clinic Award, and her picture book *Grasshopper to the Rescue* was a Junior Literary Guild Selection. She resides in Meredith, New Hampshire.

About the Advisor

ALLA V. KULAGINA, Professor of Russian Folklore at Moscow State University, was born in the Russian Far East in Primorskii Territory (*krai*). She is a renowned folklorist who teaches courses in folklore and leads her students on yearly folklore expeditions to Russia's remote areas to collect songs, tales, spells, anecdotes, and other folklore genres. She specializes in the ballad, lyric songs, *chastushki*, and the folktale. She has an impressive list of publications. It includes *The Russian Folk Ballad* (*Russkaia narodnaia ballada*, 1977); *Chastushki from Nerekhta* (*Nerekhtskie chastushki*, 1993); a folklore textbook entitled *Russian Oral Folk Art* (*Russkoe ustnoe narodnoe tvorchestvo*, 1996); and a collection of lyric songs entitled *Urban Songs, Ballads, and Romances* (*Gorodskie pesni, ballady, romancy*, 1999), which she co-authored with Professor F. M. Selivanov. She and A. N. Ivanov compiled a two-volume collection of wedding laments and ritual songs entitled *The Russian Wedding* (*Russkaia svad'ba*, 2000).